VOICES
of
TWO AMERICANS

*Overseas in the 1920s
Work and Adventures*

EMILY GEYMAN

Voices of Two Americans
Overseas in the 1920s
Work and Adventures

Emily Geyman

Ingram Spark Edition

Copyright 2022 by Emily Geyman

Softcover
ISBN: 978-1-882625-06-2

Library of Congress LCCN: 2022913460

No part of this publication may be reproduced, stored in a retrieval system, or transmitted in any form or by any means, electronic, mechanical, photocopying, recording, scanning, or otherwise, without the prior written permission of the author.

Postage stamps on cover are from the author's 7th grade collection.

GUS Publications
Friday Harbor, WA 98250

email: oatmeal@rockisland.com

DEDICATION

To *Two Americans,* Harvey and Roberta, the parents of my brother, David, and myself. They created a home of love and happiness with values of caring about others, a work ethic, a respect for persons different from ourselves and a world perspective. In the 1920s, they each had wanted to do good in the world and have adventures. The Y.M.C.A. and Y.W.C.A. gave them this opportunity.

To the leaders of the Y.M.C.A. and Y.W.C.A., founded in England in the mid-1800s, who supported Christianity and the Christian belief of helping people wherever and whatever their needs might be. And to the vision of leaders who adapted programs and created new ones for young people to address changing needs in their communities and evolving global challenges.

VOICES
of
TWO AMERICANS

Overseas in the 1920s
Work and Adventures

Contents

Preface 5

Prologue 7

HARVEY
   Russia 1919-1921 9
   The Interim 67
   Bulgaria 1922-1924 71

ROBERTA
   Japan 1926-1930 131

Epilogue: Next Steps for Harvey and Roberta 257

Y.M.C.A. and Y.W.C.A. 1920s and 2020s 261

Acknowledgements 265

Appendix 266

Bibliography 267

About the Author 269

PREFACE

I invite you to travel to another time and place and share the lives of two young Americans who chose to immerse themselves in cultures very different from their own. They learned new languages and made new friends who, with mutual respect and goals, together achieved significant accomplishments.

This book originally was to be for our family. As I read and re-read the letters from my parents, however, I realized that there are others who would appreciate gaining insight and perspective on diverse cultures—not from a history book but from observations and experiences of individuals.

Join Harvey and Roberta in the 1920s, before their marriage, as they independently boarded ships and crossed oceans to countries quite unknown and hear them tell of their day-to-day work and adventures.

About the Letters in this Book

This book is composed primarily of the letters of Harvey and Roberta, and excerpts from them, sent to family and friends "back home" in the United States who fortunately saved their letters. My brother David and I inherited this collection.

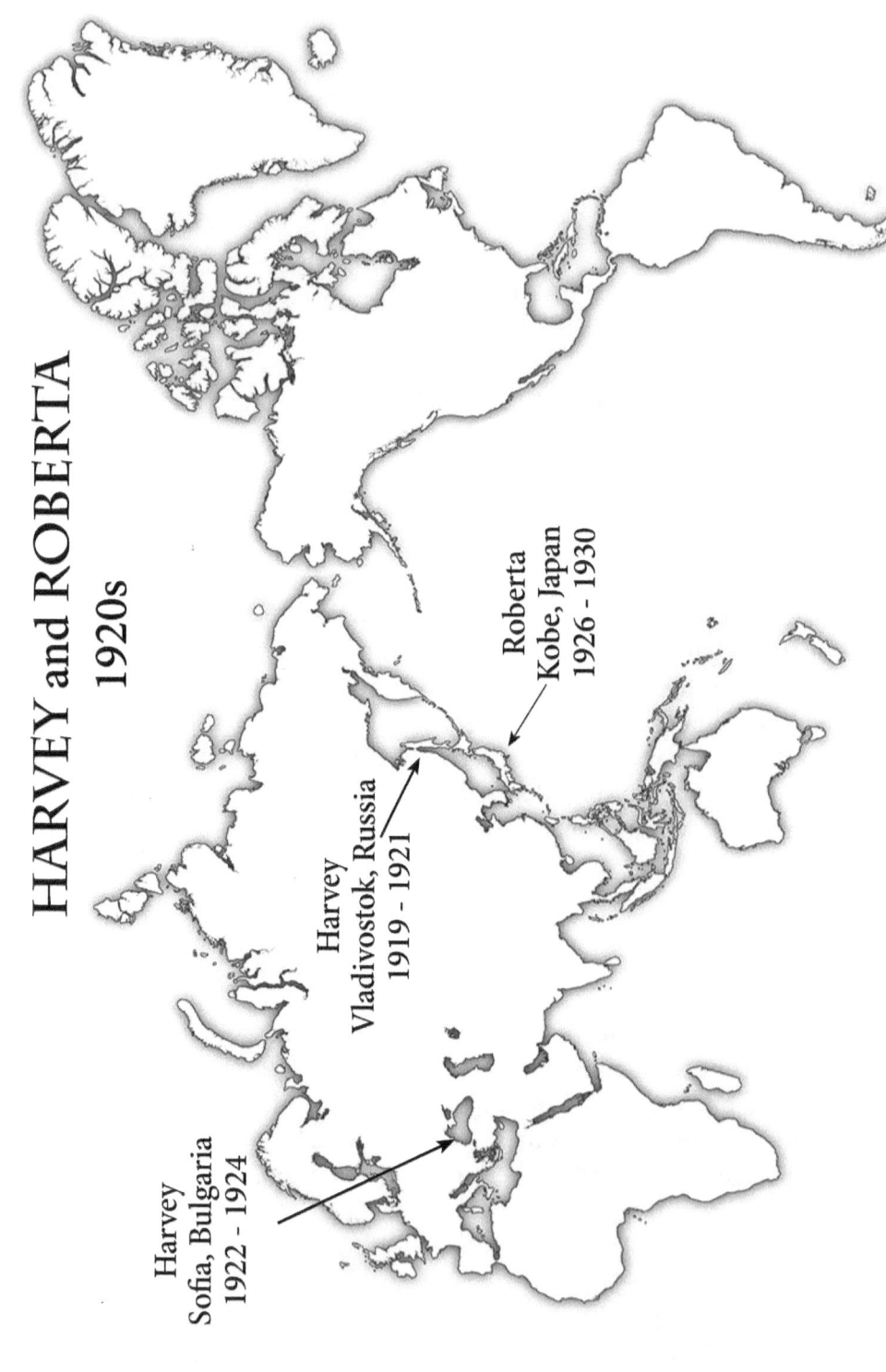

PROLOGUE

Who?
Harvey Smith graduated from the University of Wisconsin in Agriculture in 1911. He was working in Michigan as a resource for farm families and organizing 4-H clubs when he accepted an offer in 1919 from the Y.M.C.A to be a Secretary (Program Director) to develop a 4-H type program in Vladivostok, Russia. In 1922 he directed an innovative Y.M.C.A. trades school in Sofia, Bulgaria, for young (ages 18-25) Russian refugees.

Roberta Anderson graduated from the University of Iowa in 1924 with an English major. Her older brother worked in Asia and Europe with the Y.M.C.A. and she too wanted to travel. On the Y.W.C.A. campus council and familiar with their programs, she applied for a job. After orientation in New York City, she was appointed a staff member of the Grand Rapids, Michigan, Y.W.C.A. while waiting for an opening abroad.

Why?
A desire to do good in the world and to have adventures.

How?
How did these two Americans meet? Harvey returned to Grand Rapids, Michigan, after his work in Bulgaria. Roberta's brother, Paul Anderson, on the Y.M.C.A. staff in Europe, had become friends with Harvey. When Paul learned his sister was in Grand Rapids as a Y.W.C.A. Secretary, he suggested that Harvey call her. A romance ensued but Roberta wanted an adventure before "settling down" with anyone so she accepted a Y.W.C.A. offer to work in Kobe, Japan. Four years of letters and Roberta's return culminated in their marriage.

Contemplate Communication in the 1920s.

Cell phones, computers, and emails did not exist so the way to keep in contact with friends and family was to write letters —by hand or on a manual typewriter.

If Americans were living abroad, letters were sent by ship to and from the United States. There was no Air Mail; letters took 10 or more days to cross the oceans.

Television did not exist so it was by radio, newspapers and magazines that people got national or international news. Telephone calls could only be made in homes or businesses or in free-standing telephone booths in cities and towns.

Traveling was by car, boat, train, bus or in some rural areas by horse and buggy. Commercial airlines did not exist. People crossed oceans by ship.

About Y.M.C.A. & Y.W.C.A. Staff

The title, Secretary, was used to describe the staff positions of Harvey and Roberta and others in the Y.M.C.A. and Y.W.C.A. Their work was similar to the work of Program Directors in other community organizations.

HARVEY IN RUSSIA

HARVEY'S PASSPORT
RUSSIA 1919

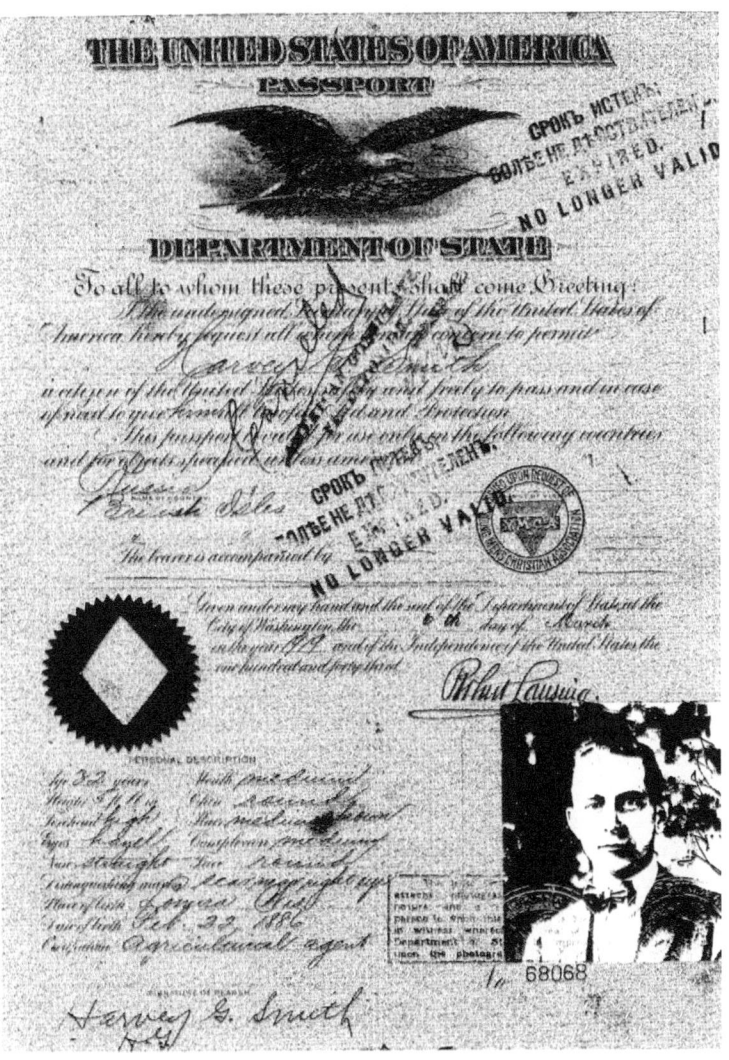

HARVEY in RUSSIA
1919-1921

Contents

Who is Harvey?..13

On the Way to Russia..15

Map of Russia 17

Russia - Perspective 19

The Mayak /Y.M.C.A in Russia 20

Arrival in Vladivostok. 21

North to Khabarovsk.. 27

West to Irkutsk..31

Living in a Boxcar & the Russian Revolution 33

On the Trans-Siberian Railway 37

Return to Vladivostok 41

    Learning Russian/Living With a Russian Family......46

    A Samovar..47

    Garden Clubs and Politics...49

    New Position: Senior Secretary/Trip to Peking 54

    Speech in Russian & Y.M.C.A. Thriving....................58

    Going Home: Gift of Russian Icon 63

Brandon Boy Did Good Work in Russia................................64

WHO IS HARVEY?

Harvey Smith, born in 1886, grew up on a small dairy farm near the town of Brandon, Wisconsin. Harvey, his sister and three brothers worked on the family farm. Church activities were a major source of recreation, and Harvey remembered having to leave early from good times with friends "to go home and milk the cows." His parents valued education for their sons and daughter; while one son decided to have his own farm, the others all finished college.

Harvey graduated from Brandon High School at age 18 and lived at home for three years while teaching in a one room school to earn money for college. He went to and from school with a horse and buggy and started a fire in the wood stove on winter mornings to heat the classroom.

At the University of Wisconsin in Madison, the College of Agriculture, his major was Horticulture (no more milking cows for him!). Harvey graduated in 1912 and became Agricultural Exension Agent in Alpena County, Michigan. He was a resource for farmers, worked with farm women in food preservation, for example, canning fruits and vegetables (home freezers did not exist) and developed a 4-H program for boys and girls.

Harvey and his students

Later he worked in Grand Rapids, Kent County with similar responsibilities. In 1919 Harvey accepted an offer from the Y.M.C.A. to work in Vladivostok to develop a 4-H type program with youth to create vegetable gardens and grow food for their families who were living in poverty.

Harvey's Letters

The letters that Harvey wrote to his parents in Brandon, Wisconsin, sometimes appeared in the small-town newspaper, *The Brandon Times*. It was very unusual to have a young man from Brandon working abroad in those years so Harvey's letters were considered newsworthy. A letter Harvey wrote to his younger brother, Wyman, was also in *The Brandon Times*.

Most of the letters we have were to his older brother, Andy, and his wife Leona, in Utah. They had a chicken ranch south of Salt Lake City which was their livelihood, and Andy saved many of Harvey's letters.

Note:
Harvey's letters in this book, and recollections of his experiences, are all in quotation marks.
Background information and explanations which I have written are without quotation marks or within boxes.

ON THE WAY TO RUSSIA
Michigan to San Francisco
By Train

"April 15, 1919
Dear Andy and Leona,
Yes I am on my way to the land of Russia. Isn't it strange that I should be going so far when there is so much to do in America.

I am glad I am going even though there is much uncertainty ahead. It is all adventurous. Many new experiences will develop and I will look forward to opportunities for the development of my leadership and executive ability. I need this if I am ever to do big things when I come back.

Tolstoi set himself the task to do worthwhile things all the time. Why can't I do likewise and succeed? I am on my way and how I will try. When I come back I shall have a long story to tell you of Russia. I hope I will be given opportunity to travel from one end of Russia to the other, to live with peasants and anyone who will help me to know Russia as it really is and to learn something for the U.S. I am setting myself a big task but that is the way it is, is it not. I hope you are glad I am going. I need your support.

I am sorry I could not get away early and come around by Sandy. I suppose you think I am not much of a brother. No, that isn't it at all. Our whole expedition has been more or less uncertain and so there was no possible way of my getting away. I had so much responsibility in getting things together at the last minute - in fact some is still getting. Anyway I am here and on my way - sorry not to see you in your home. If I ever do get back we will have some real time will we not? I must tell you that this first big trip is most wonderful for me.

I am in a party of twelve and this makes our trip more interesting. The thing that I am enjoying more than all else is a closer contact with the mighty forces of nature.

When one sees towering away into the sky rock and strata in the perpendicular rather than flat, as we know it back home, we can realize for once at least that there have been mighty forces at work in the old earth and if they have been, then they must be there still. If they are in the earth then they must be in us and it is up to us who can think to use them for the good of all. That is a bit of philosophy.

Some of the interesting things that I have seen are the extensive prairies. We traveled all day Sunday and Monday through the land of production. What a land it is. It looks so rich and the people have the expression of determination in their faces

Now today I have seen some more grand, immense, beautiful, majestic, sublime, sad, delicate, inspiring scenery than I have ever seen before in my life . . .

I wonder what you and other people think when they see all of Nature's activities like here. All my senses seem to be affected, and not only my sight as I had thought. I am glad of it. I have seen the highest point along the line - it is about 15,000 feet. Castle Mountain (14,279') and Cathedral Mountain (13,944') were well named. I thought of Balder, the God of Greek mythology, and the Greeks looking somewhat abashed from their shrines when they saw these.

Don't feed the chickens on this. It won't help them to lay eggs. I must stop and write other letters. Write me Vladivostok, Siberia, American Y.M.C.A. c/o American Consul.
      Your brother,
       Harvey"

RUSSIA

Siberia is the area of Russia east of the Ural Mountains extending to the Bering Sea and Pacific Ocean and south to Iran, Afghanistan, China, Mongolia and Korea.

The cities where Harvey worked—Irkutsk, Khabarovsk, Harbin and Vladivostok—are on the map.

1917-1922 in RUSSIA

Two revolutions at Petrograd (St. Petersburg) in 1917 significantly changed the government of Russia:
1. The February Revolution caused Tsar Nicholas II to abdicate and a Provisional Government was established.
2. The October Revolution, led by Lenin, challenged the Provisional Government, and the Bolsheviki became the Communist Party.

To stay in power, Lenin had to cope with opposition in western Russia, from Poland to the Crimea, so did not have the military strength to immediately move east.

After the October Revolution, diverse groups competed for power including the Reds, who supported Lenin, the Whites, who with Allied support opposed him, and the anti-communist Cossacks in Siberia. The Whites were popularly associated with the ideology of the past while the Communists spoke of a new path for the future. Political activity in Siberia also included the Far Right and Far Left, and armed conflict among political groups was not uncommon.

Most Siberians were apathetic unless their personal property or lives were threatened, and most appeared to try to survive and let the political groups fight it out among themselves. A complicating factor was the continued presence of Japanese armed forces in the Vladivostok area. When they withdrew in 1922, the Reds formally established Communism as the government of all Siberia.

Reference:
Vladivostok Under Red and White Rule:
Revolution and Counter Revolution in the Russian Far East
1920-1922 —Canfield F. Smith

The MAYAK /Y.M.C.A. in RUSSIA

Background

James Stokes, an American on the board of the International Y.M.C.A., met a Russian nobleman, Baron Fredericks, in 1898 in Paris who was impressed with the Y.M.C.A. program there. At his invitation Stokes went to St. Petersburg, met with him and others, and they initiated a request to the Tsar for a new organization for young men.

In 1903 the Society for the Promotion of Intellectual and Physical Development of Young Men, which became known as the Mayak or Lighthouse (English translation), was approved. Its purpose was to provide practical assistance to the young men who arrived to work in the city and needed support in adjusting to their new surroundings in positive ways.

By August 1917 over 3500 men were participating in the programs of the Mayak in St. Petersburg. Stokes had funded a new building and gymnasium; Russian and Y.M.C.A. staff shared social, recreational and educational program responsibilities.

In 1918 Lenin officially closed this Mayak/Y.M.C.A., nationalized the building and took its assets.

1919-1921 in Vladivostok

In 1919 the Y.M.C.A. requested and received permission from the Provisional Government in Omsk to continue their diverse work in eastern Russia. The Mayak and Y.M.C.A. worked together in Vladivostok through 1921.

Reference:
The American YMCA and Russian Culture —Matthew Lee Miller

ARRIVAL in VLADIVOSTOK

"June 18, 1919
Dear Andy and Leona,
   I have just had dinner here in this far away country. I wish you had been here with me or to be more effective I wish I had been with you eating a juicy chicken dinner. I haven't had a chicken dinner since I have been here, and while one may tire of them like a Methodist dinner nevertheless I would be glad to take a good shank well browned in my hand and in true style eat the choice morsel.

   I was happy to have your multitudinous letter reach me with one from Wyman. I don't care how many copies you make with your labor saving device so long as you do not soon conclude that an ordinary American Typewriter will run itself. I am sure this advice you will take seriously and become an intimate friend of your writing machine.

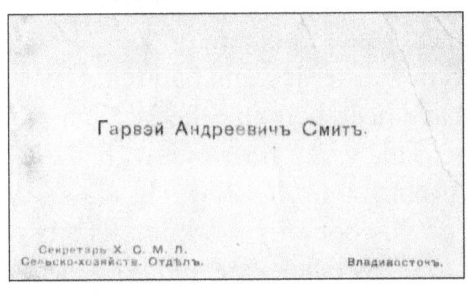

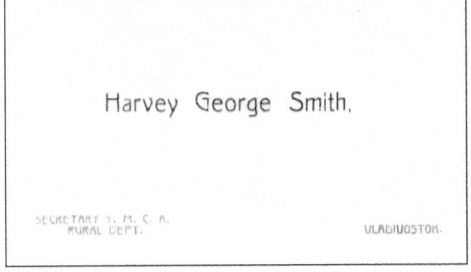

This is a great country and interesting. I have learned a lot since I have been here and yet it is so little compared to the unknown information that is out in and among the customs of the people. These people are so different than we are and yet they are so human and so much like us.

I have learned to know so many splendid people and I wish I knew more. I miss not knowing the language. There is much to learn of the agriculture of this country.

I wish I could describe the scenery here. I almost dare to say that your beautiful Utah is not in a class with us here. I went over to Russian Island Sunday and there I was more than amazed at the wonders of nature. The flowers grow wild and in their freedom seem to enjoy it and yet they welcome those who come and stroll at their side and I'm not so sure but some are willing to give their life to help make humanity more human.

I was on a picnic yesterday and had real U.S. coffee for the first time since I have been here in Siberia. Picnics are as joyful here as back home. This was a little one with six in the party and was made over a gruntling fire.

Now I must go on about my work in this city of wonders. I wonder how all the new chicks are and how they play under the same sun that I am now going to get warm under.

Your brother,
Harvey"

> This letter was published in *The Brandon Times*.

Letter From Russia.

Written by Harvey J. Smith to his brother Wyman.

Vladivostok, May 21, 1919.

"Just two weeks ago today I landed upon the shores of this new and unknown country. And what joy to see here the imprints of modern civilization. No, not quite an American city, but one with long ear marks of that which might be American or could soon become such. There are street car lines, electric lights that are on most of the time, but off once in a while in the evening, or if not off give not the radiance of brilliancy, but rather the glimmer of the star or the glow of the setting sun. Automobiles hurry the streets as if they were mad and little know where they next stop, but I suppose they do. I cannot leave this autonomous subject without saying that there are Fords, Cadillacs, Packards, Bnicks. Mitchells, Overlands and several other common American machines in the array that makes us look for the tall timbers when the squak comes out of the distance near or far.

The common mode of reaching a new point is to walk, to the office or mess or down town or to the "hut" and most any place you want to go. It is not difficult to practice this method of advantage, for I learned it in my childhood and because I am in a new country is no reason for me to learn over the things that come by natural inheritance.

But you do want to know that this is a beautiful city. It stretches itself out to an extreme thinness in many places but over all it is about eight miles long and a half to a mile wide. This is not a smooth plane, but rather an endless expanse of hills and valleys and now can you see one hundred fifty thousand people at the every day duties of life, going and coming, at play and at work, each helping to make the world go a bit faster than the day previous. And that is where I stopped to go for a walk with one of my best new chums. Now am back and tired as I am, I shall wait for the "old Orb" to wake me into the beauty of another day. I am physically tired for the first time in many a day, and thus I should sleep one of those sweet sleeps that comes to those who work with their hands.

CITY of VLADIVOSTOK

In the 1800s Vladivostok was the major seaport for Russia in the east and in 1872 became the main Russian naval base on the Pacific. The population then grew and by 1914 had increased to 100,000.

In 1891 construction of the Trans-Siberian Railway began in Moscow and by 1916 it reached across Russia to Vladivostok. During World War I, Vladivostok was the chief entry port for military supplies from the United States to Russia which were sent west on the railway.

Following Lenin's 1917 revolution in western Russia, thousands of intellectual and cultural opponents of Lenin moved east to Vladivostok. They established two theatres, several symphony orchestras and in 1920 the Far Eastern State University was founded.

Vladivostok Harbor in the 1920s

MAYAK/Y.M.C.A. in VLADIVOSTOK

> When Harvey arrived, he expected to begin garden clubs. However, work of the Mayak/Y.M.C.A. was focused on the gym, films, games, books and food for refugees, prisoners of war and American and Japanese military in the area.

Review from the International Y.M.C.A. Committee of New York published 1921 in *The Brandon Times:*

"When Smith reached Vladivostok there were still so many prisoners of war, refugees, and soldiers and sailors there that the work was carried on almost entirely in their behalf. Literally thousands of men passed daily through what was called the International Hut. In one period of nine months, three quarters of a million men made use of that hut and its facilities. These men represented many nationalities . . .

It was at Vladivostok that for some months were the Czecho-Slovakian soldiers, who, interned by the Bolsheviki after the Russian collapse, fought their way through to the Siberian Railway, took it over, and finally reached the Pacific coast. The Y.M.C.A. had been with these troops through their strange journey across Siberia to the sea. It went with them also on their trip from Vladivostok by water around to the Mediterranean and shared with them their remarkable home-coming."

3 Story Building is The International Hut

MAYAK/Y.M.C.A. (continued)

> A few months after Harvey's arrival in Vladivostok, he and another secretary traveled north to Khabarovsk to look at the potential for starting programs there.
>
> He then refers in a letter to a change of policy and in November traveled to Irkutsk in central Siberia with plans for working there.

Czechoslovakian Soldiers in Vladivostok

"There were in Russia betwen 40,000 and 50,000 Czechoslovak prisoners of war, forced soldiery of the Austrian Arm, who had freely surrendered to the Russians, unwilling to fight for the Austrian throne. The Czech soldiers, armed and officered, were on their way out of Russia via the Trans-Siberian and Vladivostok, headed for the western front under arrangements made by the Czech government in exile . . .

Progress was painfully slow. Some units spent two months in freight cars covering a distance which should have taken no more than two days. Disputes flared. The Bolsheviks tried to propagandize the Czechs to stay in Russia and fight for the Revolution. One thing led to another.

On May 14 a row broke out at Chelyabinsk in the Urals between Czech soldiers and Hungarians, also prisoners of war. The local Soviet arrested several Czech soldiers and on May 17 the Czechs marched into town, released the prisoners, and disarmed the Red Guards. Within a week the Czechs had moved to the offensive and were taking over one Siberian town after another."

Black Night, White Snow Russia's Revolutions 1905-1917
—Harrison E. Salisbury

NORTH to KHABAROVSK

"September 9, 1919
Dear Andy and Leona,
    . . . I have been here in my new place for about a month today. I am now about 500 miles north of Vladivostok on the Amur river. This is a beautiful city with a population of about fifty thousand people. It is located on the river Amur which is the sixth largest river in the world. Boats come from the ocean to this port and others go up the river a large number of miles. I should say about a thousand from here and we are almost that far from the mouth. You can readily see that we are not on some little trout stream but on a real river like you and I would not wish to swim in our short life.

    This city has fine people in it. Mr. Donan, who is here as secretary with me, and I are meeting them every day and are enjoying them immensely. They are so hospitable and courteous. I sometimes wish we were more so. In our hurry to get things done, which is a pure U.S. trait, we forget some of the more pleasant courtesies which should be ours.

    My one handicap to complete enjoyment here - the language. If I were able to chat along at my usual rate in good American I would be sitting on top of the world as we say.

    The city has fine broad streets paved of stone. The main street is the one where our office is that is better than the others. Then the city park is beautiful. It is located along the bank of the river and gives the people a place in which to enjoy their spare moments with much satisfaction . . .

I do know that there is a splendid central bath or several for that matter where one can go and get a real bath. I have my bath regularly once a week as do the Russians here.

I have spent at least an hour studying the school system. I have been getting a little information each week almost, but I have had a real job finding the man who could give me concisely and accurately the whole story . . .

I am not sorry for a minute that I am here. I am sorry that I have so little education. I wish I were a specialist along several lines. I shouldn't say that I haven't a good education for I have. If I had funds at my disposal it wouldn't be long and I could help a lot of these splendid people along a number of lines. I know some of the things they need and I also am learning a good deal of the needs of the people. Perhaps what I learn now will be of considerable use in one or two years if I stay here that long.

You might be suprised to hear me say that I think I am getting a real education here and for that matter I believe equal to spending another year at some university, the only difference being that here I do not get a degree but experience, and if we can agree with John Dewey that education is life itself and not training for life, my time will have been well spent. Then there is more than that - I will have given a little service and I hope before I return, a great deal. I am positive of one thing that no one wishes to do so more than I.

If all goes well it will be very possible that I will be able to do some work like boys' and girls' club work over here. I surely like these youngsters and in my mind they are ready to do just the thing that thousands of our boys and girls are doing.

Well so the world moves on and as it does and one sees all that it is possible to see here it makes one stop and realize that there may be millions of individuals in the world but no one has any great effect in changing fundamental laws but that the greatest good to all can come only as we adjust ourselves to these findamentals.

And should I go on, you would soon say well some philosopher has sprung up in the Smith family and as yet I am not ready to make such appearance about the stage of the Smith family, although I hope to add a bit of such activity to the other attributes that make me what I am . . . Tell me all about the farm and chickens . . . I need to keep up to date for when I return I do not wish to talk like a missionary.

If you don't know what to do just be like the good Samaritan and send a letter on its way to Siberia.

Good night, Harvey"

Letter From Russia.

The following letter from Harvey Smith, who is in Russia, to his parents, Mr. and Mrs. Andrew Smith, will be of interest to the Times readers:

Y. M. C. A., Harbovsk, Siberia,
Aug. 18, 1919.

Dear Parents:—Do you see what has happened? You are getting a letter from a new place. I can tell you I am mighty glad to be able to write you from a new place? I am now about five hundred miles north of Vladivostok on the Amur river. It took the larger part of two days to get here. The traveling was fine and most enjoyable. I saw a lot of new things and most interesting scenery.

The customs of the people in traveling are somewhat different than with us. For example at each place or station stop, most of the people or at least a large number of them, would hurry out to get their tea kettle filled with hot water for tea which they always make enroute. It is very customary to carry a teakettle, make "chi" and have lunch on the train. To add to the lunch each person can visit the venders who have little booths a short distance from the steaming hot water boiler.

I have only been in this city for three days and in that time I have learned more of Russian people than all the time I have been here. These people are more than splendid and have been extremely courteous to us. In the hotels, and restaurants we are excellently treated and are able to get very well prepared food. We have difficulty ordering our meals at times but the experience is well worth the bother. Very few people speak English here. Then my good friend and I were invited into two Russian homes today. What a pleasure it was. I suppose we considered it so big an event, for in all the time that we had been in Vladivostok we had had no opportunity to visit and become acquainted with Russian people. I cannot tell you of all the interesting things that happened, but this I know will interest you—we were served tea and the national Russian cake at one home, and tea and raspberries in another. I am a converted tea drinker, only drank seven glasses of tea today.

WEST TO IRKUTSK

The Y.M.C.A. had planned to establish rural work in western Siberia near Omsk. The Comunists had taken over Omsk, however, so staff stopped at Irkutsk.

"November 22, 1919
Dear Andy and Leona,
    I am sending you my Christmas Wishes, for should I delay longer they would be very late and I fear now that I have waited too long. I thought about Christmas quite awhile ago for thoroughly had given up hope of ever getting West. Then all at once there was a change of policy and before I knew it I was on my way to the center of Siberia. And here I am happy as I can be, for it is a place, a city that is really quite Russian. I am getting a bit acquainted and hope to be more. Would that I might get as well acquainted as up at Khabarovsk where I was before coming here.

Letterhead of Irkutsk Y.M.C.A. Stationery

    This is a great country to be in for a while. I am getting an experience that should make me better and bigger. I never knew what it would mean or could mean to anyone to travel in a new and strange land. The customs, manners, mode of life is quite different than ours and yet life seems to go on.

The latest news from the front is that Omsk has fallen. Then there are many rumors of what has happened but none of them are authentic. It does make it interesting to be here and see the effect that rumors have on people, how they act, etc. And we are driving on making big plans for hard work. I hope that everything permits us to go on and that we will not be ordered to leave here.

How I wish I might be spending Christmas with my dear relatives. It seems strange to be so far away from them all, way out in the world with just plain folks. But I do want you to have a Merry, Merry Christmas this year. And could you get a birds eye view of this suffering nation you surely would be glad that this wonderful day of all days has brought you so many joys. And so I wish you the most wonderful Christmas of all the years and that you may have many of them. I hope to be back by next year to sit at the family table somewhere.

That won't be long for time flies and I don't seem to catch it by the forelock.

        Merry, Merry Christmas
           from Harvey"

A BOXCAR and the REVOLUTION

The Y.M.C.A. remodeled boxcars for temporary living accommodations for secretaries in towns on the Trans-Siberian Railway. It apparently was uncertain how long Harvey would be in Irkutsk so this was his residence.

"January 9, 1920
Dear Andy and Leona,

Were you to come over and just for a minute stick your nose out of the door you would at least say it was cold. This is one of those quiet days when you are about convinced that it can't get much colder. I have been out most of the day and like an old "Lumber Jack" from Michigan didn't mind it very much. Since I have gotten into my car and sort of tried to get real warm toasty like, I have begun to feel that maybe it was cold today.

Have you ever lived in a boxcar? No I know you ain't and you don't want to - take it from me, he said with some little experience. But then it is quite the go around here and one doesn't mind it after all. You see I always figure that it is wise to build a house on solid rock (that is what the Bible says too) if you're going to stay. Reckon I ain't going to be here very much longer, however.

But I must tell you a bit more of this extravagant home. In the first place the wall used for support is consolidated into an axle, two of them with wheels at either end and neither the axles or the wheels are much on keeping out the cold, so far as I can see. Yes, you can see clean under the car! Then the car rocks now and then but usually when you want to sleep and then it wakes you up instead of putting you to sleep. But things go sort of upside down here so we will let the thing go on. But a little closer examination.

    We enter through the front door and back door at the same time. You don't mind do you. That is in the winter. In the summer they are separate. The first thing we see is the kitchen. In it is a large brick stove on which to do the cooking, then a table, wood, coal, the latter two are much needed, and then shelves for food. This is really the pantry and if you prefer we will call it such, although we are still in the same room. Right back of you is the coat rack, just like on the farm we have the coat rack right back of the door. Right in the middle of this rather elongated room is a nice shiny white oilcloth. This is the dining table. Oh, you thought it was a plain board table did you. We have quite a bit of style about us even though we are quite away from home.

    And now we enter the living room. Notice my afghans for my bed. I guess they were knit back in the states somewhere. They surely are beautiful aren't they. And right here in the corner is a little Russian stove, not very large that is true, but a good heater. It keeps fire all night and I sleep as near as I can to it. We don't happen to have rocking chairs to sit on but we do have some peasant made cane chairs with a little spring in them. I am sitting on one of them now. (If you don't mind I'll show you how the stove works. I have it roaring a little now so that I won't get cold.) Then I have two tables here and around me a lot of books. Now do you see how I live in a boxcar. There is one thing I forgot to tell you that in this room, every Saturday like back on the farm, I have a bath.

    Meals are served quite regularly, breakfast at nine, oatmeal and toast, jam rarely and slapjacks, dinner at one when I am home and supper in the evening about six or seven. I am hungry at six usually but quite often have to wait until seven. Like tonight - for tough beefsteak. I have a cook who takes care of the car fairly well although not over anxious to do much scrubbing.

This is a peculiar country but never stops being interesting. I have about concluded to spend the rest of my life here after I return to the USA.

It was Christmas morning when more usually interesting events started. Part of the town had become revolutionary. That night none of us ventured out and during the next ten days fighting was going on in at least some part of the city. I just want to tell you that things were a bit noisy and you just didn't feel altogether safe of your life. Finally the day for a truce came.

The allied commissions wanted to get out of town. There was a lull for first twelve hours and then twelve more. The trains got out and then we thought the worst would follow. Me sitting right near the line of fire in my box car behind a plain board fence. A little chilly in the blood and not altogether pleasant.

But on the following morning, instead of fighting again, all was quiet and the news came that the social revolutionaries had won. So now everything is quiet and from all appearances may be so. Stores are open again and business is running as usual. We have sent out a considerable group of our people and the balance will be leaving before very long. I expect to be on my way to the East within several weeks, although I would really prefer to go the other way . . .

Keep the chickens in good running order . . . I'll want one if I come back that way you see.
       Dosvidonia,
        Harvey"

Trans-Siberian Railway 1920s—Steam Locomotive

ON THE TRANS-SIBERIAN RAILWAY

At Verkni Udinsk – a stop between Irkutsk and Vladivostok

"January 28, 1920
Dear Andy and Leona,

 . . . You know I haven't had a letter from anyone for so long, I was beginning to get wild and wonder if I hadn't better turn around and go the other way where things are as interesting as here and I am inclined to think more so.

What should I tell you of all the interesting things is quite a problem. Wish you were here so I could waft gentle breezes in your ear. I am so filled up with what is going on around me that I almost hanker to get back and just calmly and deliberately open up to some of the facts that seem to be establishing themselves.

Before I get very far I should surely answer your questions. Apples, ganos - you should have coals heaped on your head for mentioning such a word. The only way I can see that apples would grow here is to have a new variety that would grow out of a glacier or likely drill a hole through the earth and slide a few through.

We have plenty of bread but the people don't. I can tell you about a little incident that happened the other day.

As we stopped at a station I saw large piles of wood and thought that it being so close to our car we might get some put in at once. So I had my two men who are with me ask politely if we could get wood. First one looked up and then the other of the sturdy, large muscular women and several youngsters who were piling wood. They appeared not to hear until one finally in her clear pure Russian way said "Kleb" (Russian for bread) and at once she was joined by her woman workers.

Who could refuse people like these bread under such conditions. For the barter of bread for wood you should have seen the real smiles as they came out of their hungry souls. I suppose all these people have been living on for weeks has been "Kasha" (porridge). Bread to them was more than cake to us without a doubt.

Meat we can buy here and thus far have had a fairly good quality and plenty of it. You should have been here to eat our delicious veal roast, brown gravy and potatoes. Food like mother used to make.

If you remember how I used to roast the meat for Sunday dinner while the good people went to church. That is the kind we had here last night. (We included for supper last night my cook and interpreter, my Czech who helps me in my Czech work, the Commandant of the Czech echelon and myself.) Wasn't that a pretty good little party.

The Trans-Siberian Railway is 5772 miles in length from Moscow to Vladivostok. Tsar Alexander III approved surveys in 1886 and work began in 1891. It was built in three phases with challenges to overcome: dense forests, swamps in summer which were frozen in winter, and permafrost. Bridges and 33 tunnels were built. In some areas Amur tigers were a threat and in other areas, large gangs of bandits.

Siberian trees were unsuitable for ties, so lumber had to be imported. Rails from western Russia came by boat and also went up Siberian rivers.

Most of the work was done by men with wooden shovels who could lay 2 1/2 miles of track on a good day.

At the Paris Exhibition of 1900 the Trans-Siberian Railway displayed actual carriage and restaurant cars to entice travelers.

The Railway, with steam locomotives, was in full operation in 1916.

2019 Trans-Siberian Handbook
—Bryn Thomas & Daniel McCrohan

Milk, well most of it comes from some good old Holstein in Wisconsin I presume. How in the world these Dutch cows had enough foresight to know that a few Americans and others would want some of their life-giving products way over here in Siberia is more than I know. Somehow things seem to work out for usefulness if they are worthwhile products.

Just went out to see about dinner. You see we expect company again. Two of our secretaries have just arrived from Irkutsk and walked about 3 miles in as cold weather as we have had. They will be good and hungry without a doubt and a bit of good wholesome food won't go amiss. When I tell you what we are going to have you'll be surprised - creamed dried beef on toast, more toast and butter, sweet potatoes, blueberry sauce, coffee, some of those real chocolate mints I have just found in my Christmas package (bless your hearts), and then the smokers may "Koreae" (smoke). Now I bet you are envious. But you see if it were not for the cans made in USA we would not fare quite so well here. And those who run out of supplies and some there are surely feel it suddenly. And such is the life here in Siberia.

How I wondered what the big box might have in it and then as I pulled it apart I knew it would be interesting and have just what is most welcome in cold Siberia. A box of sweets such as I have not seen yet. Oh boy as we would say they are good. Last night I ate enough to make me sick. Now I have my fill for awhile and I should be more temperate . . .

Being way out in central Siberia made it impossible to get Christmas goodies on time and hardly did I expect any to come along for it is so difficult to get things through the mails. But out of the bottom of my heart I am as happy as a youngster and thanks many times. I hope my little Russian arrived in due time.

How long I will be here yet no one knows but the latest reports are, and we have had word from the Station Commandant, that we go out in a short time at least today. This time we will stop about a thousand versts (verst = .66 mile) from here . . . perhaps a day, then another thousand, another stop, several more days and then to Vladivostok.

This trip I'm having is a royal one for my blood. I fear that I am missing something, but I'm opening all the pores and believe me I will be soaked fairly well but not like the sponge, so I cannot move.

I wonder if I told you that I went through a Revolution at Irkutsk beginning at Christmas and ending after New Years. The city is now in control of the Soviets. The latest reports are that the industries are being nationalized in true socialistic fashion. Kolchak with his attaché of several hundred men is in the prison to which all exiles from Russia were formerly sent.

. . .You may wonder what I am going to do soon. That I cannot say but maybe I will be enroute with a Czech regiment to Bohemia or go the rest of the way around the world myself . . .

Well so long, dinner is about ready and my guests are arriving. Take good care of the chickens and the cat and don't do anything foolish . . . Keep the old machine busy, for another letter should be due soon. I read your unwritten letters but at times the words are dashed.

                        Brother,
                            Harvey"

RETURN to VLADIVOSTOK

"February/March 1920
Dear Folks,

Here I am back in Vladivostok again . . . As has been the case for the past two years to now, it is a city that is talked about. You probably hear more about it than I do over here. I was glad to get your letter with a few words in it telling me that you had heard we were safe and sound, also my Christmas message came along and brought you the cold wishes from Siberia. That is all very well for I didn't want you to worry about me. As always I am where it is safe to stay or I wouldn't be here. When it gets unbearable I'll be on my way. There is no danger of the latter, however. We all feel as safe here as if we were back in U.S.A. Now that may be unbelievable and there may be a bit more risk but we just say nechevo (it is nothing) and let it go at that.

AMERICAN YMCA — KŘESŤANSKÉ SDRUŽENÍ MLADÝCH MUŽŮ
(YOUNG MEN'S CHRISTIAN ASSOCIATION)
ČESKOSLOVENSKÝ ODBOR.

Letterhead of Vladivostok Y.M.C.A. Stationery

Now I am going to become a real Russian. I have decided to live with a Russian family to learn Russian. I have not gotten so I can carry on a real conversation as yet. The language is difficult you can guess, but one thing is certain - I am going to make one big effort to get it. I shall eat it with my meals and talk and listen.

Now with such a program if I am still unable to speak in several months, I'll just give it up and say so. The place where I am going to stay is a very good one . . . Another secretary and I are going to try our luck at this place. So far we are hopeful of reading the daily paper soon.

So far as the association is concerned things are a little unsettled. The American army will soon be away from here, unless a small contingent stays. All the secretaries working with that section of the "Y" will also leave. Then the Czech army is going out rapidly also. The secretaries assigned to the different regiments are also leaving, they being destined for Prague, Czechoslovakia. What a great trip they will have, all the way around the world before they get back home. What wonderful sights they will see. But they are due them for the endless amount of good work they have done in their units. I sometimes wish I had taken up this interesting work.

The only men who will be left here when all the army units are removed are those who are interested in the good folks of Russia, those interested in doing something of the "Y" work we do back home. I don't know just how many that will be. I will know better when the rest are going.

I have made up my mind to stay here a while longer. I will fullfill my contract and thus get home sometime next December. I am not ready to leave here by a long ways. I am learning more of the Russian people each day. And now that I am going to be in a Russian home I ought to learn a great deal more. And then once I can intelligently read the papers and books of Russia, I know that I will have what I have been longing for ever since I have been here.

I am going along with my rural work, do what I can and help wherever I can. Most of my work will be with boys and girls. I will have headquarters here and work from here to as far West as Harbin. Of course this is the plan now. Perhaps a month from now I will be enroute home.

No one really knows just what is going to happen. I think it would be safe to say that we are gamblers on time here. Just now the betting is that we stay here, so you see I have given you a notion I will stay here. Anyway I will have interesting work.

On Tuesday of this week I appeared before a school committee and told them of my plan. There was some considerable discussion and out of it all was the approval of the plan I have been working in the U.S.A. for the past several years. I felt good and so did they.

One never knows just how or what to say here in presenting a subject. I always start out and compliment them on the good work that they have done in their way and that I am just telling them how we do our work in the U.S.A. If they approve of it all is well; if not the same feeling exists with me for I am here to give and not to dictate. That kind of an attitude is the one that pleases these people. Now I am almost of the opinion that I have found how to approach the people here on any new subject. But I must say that reservations are always mine.

Celebration of Proletarian Cultural Day—March 12, 1920

Yesterday was a great day for Russia. It seemed to me it was her Fourth of July. That is what some of the Russian people said for themselves. March 12, 1917, was the day of the revolution in Russia. Ever since then there has been toiling and trouble. The two sides that opposed each other previous to the revolution oppose each other still. This day was one in which the revolutionary side has won recognition and they took the third anniversary as one for celebrating their joy and their freedom.

The day was advertised as a proletarian culture day. Early in the morning there was life and more life in the streets. It seemed true that people had arisen this morning to celebrate. Flags, red ones were everywhere. Posters, hand-painted, were seen hanging over the entrances of the important buildings.

And then came first from one way then another, great crowds of children. What lusty voices they had and how happy they were as if all of them knew the exact meaning of the day, and no doubt many of them did. They marched to their proper place as had been ordered several days in advance. One thing was certain with the way they walked that they were going to be in the big parade. They were filled with the life of spring and the life of youth. Soon the crowds began to gather, automobiles flew here and there, companies of soldiers with their red star, the sign and color of the new army, moved into columns for the parade which was surely to be a long one. All the style, hustle and bustle that we go through in getting ready for a big parade were evident on every hand.

Soon the parade was to start. The time was set at nine o'clock but like most such festive occasions it was late. But at ten o'clock it was under way and that was good time considering so many occasions that are late in Siberia. The parts that we had seen going here and there were now together in a regular order. And it was good order. First came the mounted police for the city, then companies of soldiers, Cossacks, marines and infantry; then organizations showed their colors with large red pennants, and then came a number of Soviets, workmen, tradesmen. What a mass of school children - some in automobiles, some walking, but all happy, singing and yelling at the top of their voices. As no parade is a parade without a band so this one would have been a failure. But the bands, there were a number of them, helped to give life and spirit to the occasion.

Thus for most of half a day the parade went by and people filled the streets watching it go by. What a crowd it was. It was impossible to walk on the sidewalks, neither could one go faster than the crowd. Telephone poles had their regular load of on lookers, and every balcony or street window had heads looking out to see this mass of people celebrating.

What was interesting to me was the scarcity of policemen. But they would have had little to do. There was no crowding, no shooting, no drunkenness, but there was happiness on the face of everyone. They seemed to have come to be orderly, and each to do his part in helping to make the day successful by adding his or her part to the order of the day.

In this last word I must also remember the women. They took part in the parade as if they belonged to the new government and on the same basis and as an equal with the men, brothers, fathers, friends they carried their new responsibilities and the new spirit which they had come to celebrate. They not only marched but in the speeches of the day they too had their representative.

When the parade and the speeches were over this mammoth crowd went peacefully home - there were literally thousands of them. And at least ten thousand were in the parade. This is a day long to be remembered for it was the first celebrated throughout all Russia.

Harvey"

Harvey's Memories of a Russian Family
Written in 1957

"While I was in Vladivostok I lived with a Russian family. The family was composed of a father who had been a Colonel and his wife, a son about nine years old, the mother's sister and the mother's mother, well known in Russian family life as Babushka. The grandmother was especially interesting. She was an avid reader. She knew practically all the books by the outstanding Russian authors and besides had read a number of books on American life. She often spoke of Lincoln and wished Russia had such a man.

The life in this family appeared to me very similar to any good American family.

I must add that all of the members attended church services quite regularly. The Russian Easter Service is the great religious holiday of the year.

Several days before Easter there is great activity in the home. Cleaning and scrubbing but most important of all is the preparation of the midnight feast following the final Easter Service. I have never seen a table laden with so much food. All the national Easter foods were prepared for the occasion. The special Easter bread with the cross of Christ across the top (meaning Christ has risen), special dishes of cottage cheese and many others.

Of course tea was prepared in a samovar and one must drink much of it to satisfy the hostess."

THE SAMOVAR

Harvey made tea in this samovar and brought it back to the U.S. in 1924.

Tea is a basic part of Russian life, traditionally made in a samovar. This is a large often brass container with a smaller container in the center where charcoal is burned to heat the water around it. A small smoke-stack is usually fit on the top to create a draft when starting the fire, then removed.

When the water is hot, it is poured into a small teapot, with loose tea leaves, and placed on top of the samovar for the tea to steep. The steeped tea is strong so a small portion is poured into a cup with additional hot water poured from the spigot of the samovar, depending on how strong you prefer your tea. In the 1920s, men were served tea in glass tumblers and ladies in teacups. A dollop of jam was sometimes added to the tea.

1968 Reflections by Harvey about Garden Clubs at a School and Early Communist Influence

"I will give you a little experience we had at the time we organized the school garden clubs. After we presented the club plan one teacher stood up and said he thought the plan was wrong. He insisted that all the members should work together as if they were one gardener. The principal of the school said each member will have his or her own garden. If you want your kind of garden club you can organize your own club and find a location you will like. He did this. Only about eight or ten children followed him. We watched the leaders work with the united work program, that is working together for all.

We passed this garden each time we went to see how our club members were progressing in comparison with the group garden. Each time there seemed to be less and less interest. The end result was that our club members had excellent gardens and much usable produce for their homes.

The group garden ended up with nothing and none of the few children continued doing any work. In other words the group plan did not work at all. The leader of this group club we learned later was a communist. We never saw him after his failure with his type of garden club."

GARDEN CLUBS and POLITICS

"May 2, 1920
Dear Andy and Leona,
    Just to show you that the weather can't stop me from doing what I want to do, I am writing letters this afternoon along with several other activities . . . I have been out almost all day in the chilly wind that has been blowing mist in my face and I have enough of it. Well, I went to church, then dinner and then to a meeting of good Russian folks.
    I must tell you about this last meeting for it is quite interesting. I had been to one of the suburbs organizing a boys' and girls' garden club. Today I went back to meet the parents and tell them what the plan was and ask them to help in the work by cooperating, that they were to be interested in their youngsters and help in anyway that they could to do the most worthwhile things.
    Well you should have seen the smiles and heard the fine expressions of appreciation and the promises of help that they were ready to give to make the work of these youngsters successful. I was surprised for I had hoped that someone would come with a grouch and would try to get rid of it at this meeting. But not so.
    The meeting was wonderfully orderly and the interest was keen. Then some of the parents made little speeches telling how they were glad that I had come with this new work and that they were willing to help. Gosh it makes a fellow feel that he is helping a little when such folks get up and tell what they think of a program that comes from a foreign country.

And then the kiddies. Here they were with their happy faces and smiles ready to say hello and goodbye in their Russian way. And the boys who call several times to you when you don't see them just to have a friendly word come to them. I tell you it seems good. When I meet such people I just want to stay here all the time.

There are interesting things happening each day. I suppose from the papers you read that I am about to be killed and am in awful bad hands. Do you know that the people that I spent such a splendid day with are the people that are supposed to be so terrible. I tell you they are just folks and when they meet the right kind of folks they are ready to go ahead and do business.

I will say that they need good leaders with a bit more practical ideas than some that are advanced, but I am not ready to see all these people over here put under the red color that the papers are so anxious to do . . . The allies owe these people freedom and not fetters for the millions of men lost in the great war.

Now how are the chickens? I hope you are saving one for a fine roast and stuffing. From all appearances I will be returning by the way of San Francisco and now you can guess my first stop. You have quite a lot of time to wait yet for I expect to be here until in the fall sometime, November perhaps. I am just giving you a warning.

Hope you are feeling fine and that the chickens are helping to keep up your spirits. Don't forget to play while you are so busy. So long for this time . . .

                Your brother, Harvey"

Harvey Demonstrating How to Plan a Garden at an Orphanage

Harvey's goal was to develop Garden Clubs for boys and girls, on the American 4-H Club model, so they would learn how to plant and take care of a garden to provide food for their families. Seeds were supplied to club members.

In his notes Harvey wrote that Russians had not been preserving vegetables for winter months. He taught steam and hot water bath methods to parents and club members and commented that it was a real success.

There were 50 students in garden clubs organized through schools and 200 youth in the Garden Club of an Orphanage.

> Excerpts from letter that Harvey sent to his parents published in the *The Brandon Times*.

WRITES HOME FOLK FROM SIBERIA

Vladivostok, Siberia, Aug. 10, 1920.
Dear Folks:—I will try a little of my yellow paper on you and if you like it I may try again. This is some I took with me when I left Chicago. I have most of it yet and so am trying it out on my best friends and of course my folks. How do you like it? Hope you don't think it is an emblem of yellow with me.

My work is getting along fine, but it would get along better if I were a native and thus could speak in the Russian language. The children are fine and are as interested in their work as our youngsters are in the U. S. A. They have met with many discouragements however, and enough to make them stop their work. Have I ever told you that here the common practice is to have the pigs and the cows, the chickens and the geese and any other animals enjoy themselves on every inch of soil except that on which a house or some building is built, and at rare intervals I have even seen them run into the house to snatch a crust of bread or at least some food to satisfy their hungry bodies. Can you see a town with all the animals loose? That is what is here and what the little gardeners have to contend with. The old neighborhood cow and several pigs, or the horse turned out for the night find the greenest spots and make themselves at home. The old cow stretches her tongue out at full length to get the tender corn tops. The old hog with one root lifts the plant right out of the ground and so the corn crop is destroyed. Now you know when this happens several times it destroys all the enthusiasm and so the youngsters finally conclude, let the animals the greedy things, have it all. There are thieves around, men, women or boys, who are too lazy to work and they like to divide the rewards of labor with the industrious little workers. So it goes and now you know what a time I have keeping my little Russian youngsters interested.

CHICKENS and LEARNING RUSSIAN

"Dear Andy,

You know when I think of chickens, I always remember the little snowballs we used to pick up in our hands as kids and the chicks would pick away at our buttons getting no food but having a lot of fun and I sometimes think we had the most fun. Those were the great days of our youth. I wouldn't have missed them for a great deal. When I am way over here I let my mind run down on some of those old paths and it is fun even though I am all alone.

I am staying home from a big concert tonight just to write more letters. You see I think quite a lot of my relatives when I do a stunt like that. I need to write a dozen letters before I get through but I fear another day will be better. I have one to write to my editor friend of a Grand Rapids paper. I feel apologetic when I think of him for I have promised to write him each week. I shall do better now.

About a year ago I was thinking a lot of getting my things packed for a long trip into foreign lands. In all the time that has passed I have had a great experience and have done a little. I hope to do a lot more now and from appearances I believe I can come back feeling that I've done something that has been worthwhile.

Within a few months I hope to be able to carry on quite a fair conversation in Russian. I am going to spend half of each day at my task and I know one thing and that is not two, that your little brother is going to be able to read the papers and such other things as are becoming to Russians.

Give my good wishes to all the family . . .

Your Siberian brother, Harvey"

HARVEY APPOINTED Y.M.C.A. SENIOR SECRETARY

"November 2, 1920
Dear Andy and Leona,

Here I must write you that you will not need to prepare the fatted chicks for me as soon as you had planned. I am not going to leave here for another five or six months.

The whole business has happened because the government does not permit wives to come over here and join their husbands.

Mr. Mitchell who is now senior secretary of the city Y.M.C.A. has a wife and family back in Seattle. They have planned to join him here but cannot now. Thus he cannot stay for he has no business being away from his growing family too long a time. His wife can come to Harbin which is a Russian city but which is under Chinese control. Thus he goes there and I replace him here.

Of all our dozen or more secretaries here those who have been selecting men to fill certain places feel none of them would be able to fill the place well. Thus as a last resort they have come to me asking if I cannot stay on a little longer to help them over this condition. I of course know that it is a sacrifice on my part but I know that the work is so important that I am satisfied to stay and help out for a little longer period.

For staying I do get some little rest. I am to take a rest and go to China. I will go to Peking and Tientsin for several weeks and return. When I get back I will go out to the country and rest from my journey and then I will be ready to get into the harness for real hard work.

This evening the leaders of my garden clubs surprised me by having a special evening. They said a lot of nice things about me, about all the Garden Club work and what a fine thing it has been for Russia.

The plan will live and grow for the welfare of the people of Russia. According to all these leaders I must return and carry on this work until the leadership here is strong enough to do the work and lead in the way they have been taught.

I shall always remember these days of this year as the richest of my life and I only hope that I may be more useful in the future.
Good night, Harve"

Harvey's Recollections about Garden Clubs and the Provincial Fair written in 1968

"With the approval of the local government we went to the schools with the similar program we had followed in the U.S. Our projects were Garden Clubs. At an orphanage we had two hundred members and at a large school over the hills in the suburbs we had about fifty gardeners. Seeds were supplied to all the members. The joy of the members and the accomplishments were almost unbelievable. As a final round up for the year's activities we had trained three club members of one club to give a canning demonstration.

In connection with a meeting of the Provincial Fair our club members gave their demonstration in a very excellent manner. I can see the little thirteen year old speaker for the club say at the end of her demonstration: Are there any questions?

The chairman with almost tears in his eyes rose hesitantly and said, These girls have shown us here what youth can do. I think it should be said for the benefit of all that the future of our country will be in the hands of the youth now growing up. We feel certain that ultimately the youth of Russia will be the hope for the some distant future."

TRIP TO CHINA

When Harvey was appointed Senior Secretary, he was offered a trip to China before assuming his new position.

"Peking November 25, 1920
Dear Pete, (Harvey's nickname for his younger brother)
. . . To give you a clearer idea of just how I passed the morning, I will continue at length. I stepped out of the "Y" and there were a dozen or more rickshaws wanting to take me somewhere. I finally selected the one who knew a little English and started off. I stopped at the photo shop and then went on to the Legation, arriving at the Internationl Banking Corporation in about ten minutes. There I exchanged money and then started off to spend it.

I stopped at a book shop but could not get any Russian books and other books were so expensive that I just thought I would have to get along without so much knowledge. But I bought a fountain pen for about four and quarter dollars American money. That is just what it cost me to drop my pen in Vladivostok. I broke the cap and none to be had here. Well I must continue on. Next I stopped at the clothing shop to buy a few ties, scarf and a pair of shoes. Did not buy the shoes on account of the price and appearance. They were Boston but not for me. Paid about twelve dollars for two ties and a silk neck scarf. The scarf is a beauty - all silk knit and from England. Thus ended my shopping.

Now my curiosity to look at beautiful rugs took me to several shops . . . The shop that I was in this morning ships to Marshall Field (store in Chicago). I guess they thought I was from there also from the number they showed me . . . I never knew the Chinese were such rug artists. All wool and almost an inch thick. You think that you are walking on real pelts. The designs are wonderful also.

But the prices of these wonderful blue and tan with slight touches of red and yellow are hardly believeable.

The price ranges from about $1.10 to $1.20 per square foot. You know I would like to bring home enough to furnish the house that I have not bought as yet. I guess I will go to one of the shops and buy one for about $20.00. Size 4x7...

I have spent two days looking at temples, the first of those in the Forbidden City. This part of the city can only be entered by pass... On top of the hill are three temples. The one at the very top... was a place of worship by the court. The others are smaller and so arranged as to give grace and symmetry to the view. The roofs of these temples were blue and gold... The wonderful designs, paintings and decorations which have remained for these hundreds of years make one wonder and stand amazed at such accomplishments long before our country ever started.

From here I went to the Winter Palace, the home of the emperor... There was the building for living, the building for entertaining members of the court, the private theatre, the home along the artificial lake, the boat landing, temples for the king's worship and all the incense burners. Such an immense expenditure of funds has never been equaled anywhere, I would believe... I little realized that the Chinese were such real geniuses as they have shown themselves to be. Last Saturday I went to the Summer Palace. The grandeur of this place equaled that of the Winter Palace.

I thought it might be more moderate but in those times I guess the kings did not think in terms of moderateness but in terms of elaborateness. I had a lunch with me and thus on the marble boat, where the early kings reveled during the hot days of summer, I drank a few hot cups of tea... All day I walked here and there up and down and around and then hardly saw all the palace... Were it not for the difficult language study I would like to be here a year or two...

A Merry Christmas to you and the folks, Harvey"

SPEECH in RUSSIAN, POLITICS & Y.M.C.A.

"April 1921
Dear Andy and Leona,
   Been a long time since I wrote you, almost forgotten when I sent the last letter. But I guess you must get most of the news from the folks anyway. I have not written so many letters and not near as many as I would like to . . . but somehow when evening and night get along, I am about tired enough to stop so don't get deep into the letter writing mood. Not only my work keeps me busy but also my Russian for I am trying more than ever to learn this language and let me tell you now that it is not an easy one to learn. The Russians say I am making great progress and I am happy.
I get along without an interpreter in great shape.

   Talking about Russian I will tell you this and I just bet your back bone will straighten up. I made a speech in Russian a week ago that was a real one. Oh I made a lot of mistakes but the Russians themselves were delighted for they got the real spirit of our work and my feeling. An interpreter always takes the life out of a speech unless he has as much enthusiasm as you have and that is what most of them lack. I ought to get a roast chicken on that when I return, had I not?

   When it comes to talking about leaving here, I am on lost ground. I have been coming home so many times that I am about to give up the plan of coming home for some time. Just today several people came to me to stay here and carry on the garden work that was so successful here last year. I ought to do it and I have a feeling in my heart that it is a plan that I ought not to stop. I ought to do it for it is one of the great forces that Russia needs. How I wish I could be more helpful in this old world. Oh if I could have more faith and more power to do the will of the Great God. How I wish the world might likewise increase its faith in the Greatest Leader, Christ for it is Christ who will see the world out of its trouble.

The Y.M.C.A. has accomplished a great piece of work here in the city already and is now just at its beginning. We have men of all descriptions members of our Association and they are mostly good. Our membership campaign ends tomorrow when we will have reports that will give us at least 550 members, the highest membership we have ever had. The enthusiasm is keen and earnest. Our program would be a credit to any Association. We are all happy about our progress.

Harvey (6th from left) and the Y.M.C.A . Soccer Team

Politically we are making a little progress. We hear people, Russians saying that peace cannot come until both sides recognize democracy, etc. It has been a hard fight for the Russians and yet they are not through. When the time will come for a better and freer life no one seems to know. One thing is certain and that is that the people must come closer to the truths of good in their practice than they have yet been. There have been efforts during the last few weeks to overthrow the government, but that has not yet been done.

We are hopeful that it will not be done for by this time the people ought to know how to evolve without further revolution.

If the other nations will get out of the way and let these folks have their way they will come out quicker and stronger. I have never had much use for intervention over here and I know that if these interveners would get out-of-the-way, the troubles would be ended more quickly. And Japan is one of the worst of the interventionists. Sad hard story this Far Eastern story. Some day it will be better . . .

For the Russian church this has been Palm Sunday. The Russian church runs on the old calendar which is 13 days behind ours. Easter is next Sunday. Last night the services in the church were very pretty. All the folks went with pussy willows which were blessed by the priest. At the time of the blessing each person was marked on his or her forehead with a cross of oil like that of old. The music was wonderful also. Now and then I like it very much but I hate a ceremony that lets people believe that religion is ceremony. Such a church must yet find itself.

I must look toward bed. I have a big day tomorrow. And by the way this was a wonderful day like we have back in the states. The grass is beginning to get green and the trees also are beginning to swell their buds for old nature who lays her plans so carefully and wisely. Well good night.

                    Your brother, Harvey"

GOING HOME

"October 11, 1921
Dear Andy and Leona,

    I hope this letter does not scare you in the least. But it may for you have not gotten one from here for a long time. Now the news that it brings is just simply this - I am coming home. I leave here in about two weeks for Japan. There I will spend about a week seeing something of that country and learning something about it. My boat leaves Yokohama on 10 of November. Thus you see at last I am homeword bound. I arrive in San Francisco on the 26 or 27 of November . . . Of course I am coming on further to Salt Lake City and you can be ready to rob your chicken family of at least one of those precious birds.

    You know it seems funny to be getting ready to leave here. I don't just feel as if I want to do it and yet I must. I want to get home and sort of take a look at myself and the friends and relatives and the U.S. and see how I fit into things after two years and a half over here. I have had a lot of good experiences and will be able to tell you all about them when I get back. You know one never knows how little he knows until he has seen a corner of the old world. It is pretty big to be able to understand. I will save the interesting parts for you and show you the pictures that go along with them . . .

    You know I am really planning to be right off again after I get back if the "Y" can continue its program. I hope to get back here and carry on an extension program if they will let me. The "Y" has gotten so popular here during the past year that I am quite certain that the movement in Russia will be a big one when the time comes which ought to be before very long.

    You will not hear from me again before I reach San Francisco. Write me there in care of the Y.M.C.A. Good wishes and with big hopes of seeing you soon.   Harvey"

Statement of Appreciation to Harvey
October 22, 1921

Dear Harvey Andreyevich,

After taking over direction of the Vladivostok branch of "Mayak" Association one year ago, throughout this entire time you never abandoned the members of the Association and dedicated yourself with great devotion and persistence to this responsible and noble work, which was related to your status as director of the Association.

As you tirelessly and successfully worked for the well-being and moral, intellectual and physical development of Russian young people you managed to develop and strengthen in them your own ideals and lead them to a life that can become normal and happy.

Therefore, please allow the members of the Association to express to you their deep gratitude for the valuable efforts you have expended and your concern for the growth and accomplishments of the Association and to wish you success in your next fruitful and cultural work.

City of Vladivostok
(With signatures of six city officials)

Icon of the Russian Orthodox Church presented to Harvey

The inscription engraved on the back of the icon:

For memory of deeply respected Harvey Andreyevich Smith from friends of society "Lighthouse" Vladivostok city 1921

> Sent in 1921 to *The Brandon Times* by the Y.M.C.A. International Committee of New York describing Harvey's work in Vladivostok.

A BRANDON BOY DID GOOD WORK IN RUSSIA

Working for the Y. M. C. A. He Helped Make Conditions Better in That War Stricken Country.

1921

The following interesting communication giving a description of the work being done by one of Brandon's well known young men, Mr. Harvey Smith, for the Y. M. C. A. in Siberia, was forwarded to the Times for publication from the International Committee of Y. M. C. A., of New York:

Goodwill vs. War

From time immemorial youth and young manhood have been in time of war the composition and fibre of the fighting organizations. They have been, as the old phase harshly but truly puts it, the "fodder for cannon;" but in recent years it has come more and more to be recognized that youth and young manhood can also be, and indeed should be, the chief instruments in progress and in rehabilitation. This is the significance of the name of the Young Men's Christian Association and of its work. It is the significance, for example, of the service of such young men as Harvey G. Smith, graduate of the University of Wisconsin of the class of 1911, who has just returned from several years work in far-off Siberia, helping to make an actuality of that respectful ministry of goodwill which will make wars less likely in the future.

Harvey's Work

Smith points out that most Americans have a wrong idea of the climatic conditions at Vladivostok. In that part of Siberia winters are not rigorous, and the spring and summer seasons are like those familiar to residents of the northern half of the United States. In common with others who have had opportunity to spend a considerable time among the Russian people, Smith has brought back a deep love for them, and a conviction of their undying hope and fundamental good sense."

...during Smith's regime the Vladivostok Y. M. C. A. came more fully into its own, and there, as also at Harbin, the work developed into that of a well-established city association with several buildings and with organized local committees. Known in Siberia as the Obshestoo Mayak, meaning lighthouse society, the Association is now carrying on in those two cities its full four-fold program—educational, physical, social and religious. The work is carried on not only by paid secretaries, but, as indicated, with the assistance of local committees.

Russian Island Boys Camp

Educational, social and religious work found fine response. A strong feature of the program was the work for boys, which included a boys' camp, on Russian Island. The camp was established there because of the disturbed condition of affairs on the mainland. Here the program of camp activities familiar to American boys was carried on and leaders trained for future work. This work for boys aroused keen interest among parents in Vladivostok.

The Y.M.C.A.

Vladivostok has shown the most satisfactory development from the standpoint of service in its civilian work. Despite occasional disturbances more or less serious, which were accompanied by armed conflict within and around the city, and despite epidemics of disease, the Association continued its work.

A Friendly Place

"It has made," says Smith, "an actual living place for itself in the hearts of the majority of the people of Vladivostok. They have learned to know it as an organization founded on and practicing principles of justice and morality. Its name has come to be known as synonomous with friendly service. To great numbers it is the only place where men can spend amid wholesome surroundings and fellowship a period of rest and recreation, mental or physical."

3rd Anniversary

"The membership is a united one. This was clearly shown at the recent third anniversary of the city Association in Vladivostok. 700 members and guests attended the celebration at the International Hut. The members include men of all types including the clergy or the Orthodox Church. Among the members are men who hope eventually to return to their native homes in Russia and these tell of their desire to take back with them the spirit of the Obo, Mayak, and help to build up similar organizations in their native cities and villages."

Basketball, Track & the Gym

Smith describes the program of work under the different departments, as for example the physical department, which aroused great enthusiasm for American methods and ideals of sportsmanship, and for American games. A basket ball tournament brought out fourteen teams, representing classes and sport clubs, although until the Y went into that part of the world no real basket ball had ever been played by the Russian boys. Under Y direction also, a big track meet was held, in which not only Y. M. C. A. teams but others representing clubs, military and private organizations, and the crews of naval vessels took part. During the first nine months of 1921, the total gymnasium attendance was above 31,000 and the participants in games and contests numbered 11,585. The gymnasium and athletic programs were conducted on the same basis as that required in the United States.

THE INTERIM

THE INTERIM

Harvey returned from Vladivostok in November of 1921 and enrolled at the University of Chicago for the Winter and Spring quarters of 1922.

It appears from his schedule that he hoped to return to Russia, for his classes included two quarters of Advanced Russian as well as history and sociology as background for his work.

```
                The University of Chicago
                    Office of the Recorder

        CLASSIFICATION                              NAME
        The Graduate School                    Harvey George Smith
                    Winter Quarter 1922
Russ.   305   Advanced Russian                      A-    1 major
Hist.   C20   Political and Social Instructions of Russia   A-   1
S.T.     38   Social Theology                        B     1
                    Spring Quarter 1922
Pol.Ec.   5   Social Control of Business             C     1
Hist.   C21   Russia since 1900                      B     1
Soc.      4   Introduction to Study of Society       B     ½
Russ.   306   Advanced Russian                       A-    1

                                         Ernest C. Miller,
                                         Recorder.
```

Harvey

"March 1922

Dear Andy and Leona,

    The finals "for the quarter" have ended. I feel quite free. Rather queer when you have one of those blame things to write you don't feel at ease until the thing is over. Now I can say "damn." My course has been mighty interesting to me. I have been brought up to date in my thinking and watch out for the world when I do start out again. If anyone happens to be in my way he is liable to tumble. That is part of my determination to accomplish a few or at least one worthwhile thing in the evolving process of earth and humanity.

    There are no immediate prospects of my going to Russia with the "Y." My own opinion is that the doors are closed to us as long as we remain capitalistic or Soviet Russia remains communistic. There is no immediate change on either side and thus I am shelved for awhile. As a result of this I have been getting feelers out on other possibilities. No $10,000 job has yet to come into sight . . .

    Your brother, Harvey"

NEW DIRECTIONS

As Harvey indicated in his letter, he did not plan to return to Russia because of the conflicting political situations in the U.S. and Russia. Later in the year he received—and accepted—an offer to direct an innovative Y.M.C.A. program in Bulgaria for young Russian refugees.

HARVEY IN BULGARIA

HARVEY in BULGARIA
1922-1924

Contents

Map of Bulgaria 74

Why was Harvey in Bulgaria? 75

1920s in Bulgaria 76

Arrival in Sofia 78

Getting the Y.M.C.A. Vocational School Started 83
    Struggles and Success 87

The School Opens 95
    Students in the Classroom 98
    Students Learn on the Job 99
    Student Life at the School 100
    Support of King Boris 101

Commencement 1923 & Summer School 1923 102

Interlude in the Rilo Mountains 105

Commencement 1924 111
    Graduates Express Thanks 117

Dinner Honoring Harvey May 1924 121
    Students Present Gift of Bench to Harvey 125

Closing of School 128

Going Home 129

BULGARIA

This map of Bulgaria was established by a conference in Constantinople in 1876-1877 and remained accurate until 1917.

As a result of World War I, changes were made in Bulgaria's boundaries but did not affect the location of Sofia where Harvey worked. Note: Constantinople is now Istanbul and Asia Minor is now Turkey.

WHY WAS HARVEY in BULGARIA?

"It struck in the form of a trade school, with three hundred imported Russian refugees from Constantinople as students and two Americans to show the faculty, also refugee intellectuals, how to prepare a project and how to make it work. It was a very serious affair . . .

The students were "intellectuals" who knew languages, not tools. But they realized they must have a trade, for the alternative was to sell cigarettes on the street, dig ditches or do other unskilled and unhappy labor. They had lived through the disorder of counter-revolution in Russia and the muck of a hundred thousand refugees in Constantinople, and were glad of a new chance . . .

Of course the School did not start with the arrival of students. The work began five months earlier with investigation of open trades and labor market, cultivation of the King and his ministers, determination of the length of course and method, and securing of equipment . . . The logic was simple: construction is booming, so teach building trades; modern utilities are wanted, so teach electrotechnics; highways are to be constructed, so teach surveying. And how might it be done in short time except by modern educational method - learning by doing . . ."

Projectitis: An Essay - Paul B. Anderson, World Service Y.M.C.A. Secretary in Europe working with Russian refugees

Location of School: Sofia, Bulgaria
Harvey Smith: Director of the School
Dr. William Orr: Educational Director

BULGARIA

Bulgaria has a history of being part of empires: Persian, Roman and Ottoman, as well as creating its own, until the Russo-Turkish War of 1877-78, called the War of Liberation by Bulgarians. That treaty recognized Bulgaria as an autonomous state, though supervised by other countries. Finally in 1908 Bulgaria became independent.
Eastern Orthodox Christianity had previously been established as had a Slavic national language. The country's cultural life included writers of prose and poetry and fine art and music academies.

1920s

The political scene, especially in Sofia, was one of controversy as diverse groups sought power. Bulgaria had sided with Germany in World War I, so was required to limit their army's size and pay large reparations. The leader of the Agrarian Party, Stambuliski, gained support of peasants and in the 1920 election won the most votes. He formed a coalition government but it resulted in controversy, not co-operation. The Agrarians supported redistribution of land and private ownership, development of co-operatives for farmers expansion of education and a progressive income tax. Urban workers and groups including the Military League, the Communists and Social Democrats opposed the Agrarians and in June 1923 a group of conspirators toppled the government including the execution of Stambuliski. The well organized urban groups gained dominance over the un-organized peasants spread over the countryside.

Political groups continued to battle, with truces and alliances signed and broken. Violent actions escalated to the bombing in 1925 of the Sevta Nedekya cathedral where 120 people died. This atrocity brought on a wave of repression which led to more controversy. In 1926 there were nineteen identifiable groups competing for dominance. The King and the military tried to keep a basic order.

The new Y.M.C.A. trades school was established in 1924 and it is remarkable that it thrived during this time of political turmoil.

Reference: *A Short History of Modern Bulgaria* —R.J. Crampton

SOFIA - Capital of Bulgaria

The dates of construction in Sofia reflect the country's political and cultural history: the Library (1878), National Assembly (1884), The Palace (1895), National Theatre (1907) Bulgarian Academy of Science (1911),and National Opera (1922). A wooden structure of the 1800s was replaced by a new Market Hall in 1911 for sale of farmers' produce. In 1913 a modern municipal public bath was built to replace the old hot mineral springs baths from Roman Empire days.

Electric trams were introduced in 1906 and routes expanded as the population reached 102,000 in 1910.

Electric trams in center of Sofia

Borisova Gradina Park was created in 1882 by Swiss gardener Daniel Neff, appointed by the Mayor. It was on 30 hectares (74 acres) with changes occurring through the years.

Churches built in past centuries were part of the city's cultural history. The Church of St. George, considered the oldest in Sofia, was built by Romans in the 4th century.

ARRIVAL in SOFIA
People - Peppers - Permissions

"Sept. 12, 1922
Union Palace Hotel
Dear Andy and Leona,

No I am not like the bear crawled into my hole for the winter. I wish sometimes that I might have so much time but that isn't given to man. Man is supposed to have lots of troubles, enough so at least he does not have much time to take a winter off in sleep.

As you can see I am in Bulgaria. It seems a long ways off to you no doubt and the queer thing to me is that it seems as far from home as Vladivostok. I guess it may be because I have not yet become accustomed to living here. Everything seems so different. You know it seems strange to travel in countries besides your own. You always are looking for something that the people do differently.

And of course there are a lot of things that they do differently and the fact is they do and don't in the least think it is queer at all. For example it is perfectly right and proper for a peasant and his wife to come into town on an old wagon drawn by a mule team. The wife may be riding or she may be whacking the oxen over the rumps with her prodding stick. She walks if the load is heavy. Now that is perfectly all right but can you see any farmer's wife poking along in a similar way in U.S.A.

And then there is another interesting custom among the women and you will see in a minute that it would not be possible for the men. The peasant women when they are dressed up to come to town or are out for a Sunday afternoon all wear their underskirts longer than the top skirt. And the underskirt of course is trimmed with beautiful handmade lace. Here it is perfectly proper and did not the women wear their skirts in such manner it would be improper. What about home even among the "Flappers."

I am studying all the customs and some day I will write a whole story of customs among the common people of Europe . . .

Sofia Market   orig Ean Forte   P. P. Morogoff   Sofia 1922

Food here is just fair. I cannot tell you much of real Bulgarian food except I know that it is prepared with a lot of hot stuff in it. Red peppers and green peppers are in abundance and it seems that peppers are in everything. I have seen a Bulgar take a big red pepper and eat it just like bread with meat or as we would with mustard. I used to have red pepper for colds and I guess you remember the stuff, Andy, and how would you like it for a daily diet. I would order a new stomach and specify that it was to be lined with non-corrodible material . . . Great stuff and I would recommend that you try a little someday when you haven't too many chickens to care for.

Well I suppose you would like to know what I am doing. I can hardly tell you for I have done so little since I have been here. I came to organize a school for Russian refugees. We have had a terrible time to get permissions to go ahead. One day we think all is well and the next day we find that the story has been reversed. So here we are sort of like the old tailor who cuts and fits and finally needs to buy a new piece of goods in order to get the suit made. I fear we will not be able to get the next piece of goods. We should know this week absolutely and if not I will pack up my little trunks and start back for Berlin and will try to keep on coming to U.S.A. I may however get into Russia.

I certainly am sorry that I missed that trip through Yellowstone Park. That must be a real trip and the camping part of it by far the most interesting. I wished the folks could have joined you but father was not well enough . . .

The folks get awfully lonesome with all of us away. They seem so alone in Brandon. They have lots of friends and the neighbors would do anything in the world for them yet it is not what they want. I hope some of us can get back a little closer to them one of these days. If I can get back and do what I hope to in Chicago I will be there in business for a while so I can at least run up and see them every once in a while. They need the warm touch of their children in these days of their lives . . .

I have about ten days off on the sick list again. I have not gotten rested from my Siberian trip and my grind at the University of Chicago. If I don't feel rested by the time I get through this time, I am going to take a year off at home and with you on the chicken ranch if you will let me. I hate to admit that I need a rest but it may be true . . .

This has gotten to be quite a long letter. You may pay me back with one as long as mine about all local affairs and the summer journey.

    Sincerely, Your brother, Harvey"

Church of St. Nicholas the Miracle-Maker

Built in 1914, this church was designed by Russian architect Preobrajenski to be similar to 16th century Russian churches. The five small domes are coated with gold and the structure of the center dome is 19 meters high.

DOING Y.M.C.A. WORK IN SOFIA, BULGARIA

The following letter was received by Mr. and Mrs. Andrew Smith, of Brandon from their son, Harvey, who left some time ago for Sofia, Bulgaria, where he is establishing a school for the Y. M. C. A.

Union Palace Hotel.
Sofia, Bulgaria,
Sept. 18, 1922.

Dear Father and Mother:

Just before bed time, I want to send you my Sunday greetings. I wish you might have been with me all day. I have had a real restful day. I am almost entirely well again and am really feeling better than I have for a long time. Some times one must get sick and make repairs before he really gets so he enjoys living. It is almost like building a new house, you get some where at least. So if you have had cause to worry a little don't any more for I am well again.

This morning I went to the little Russian church. It was just crowded to the doors. When I came to the church the minister was just giving his sermon. He told the people a lot of good things that they must do in order to live better and become better among them being, that they could not expect to make war each and every day and secure a happy peace. Peace of the real kind does not come through war he said. I tell you this because it gives some little idea of what people in this part of the world are thinking, especially Russians. The music in the church was wonderful just as I have always said Russian church music is so wonderful that when you hear it you at once feel you are in the midst of religious people and in spite of what you may want to do you are religious. I seem to find it much easier to know God through the Russian music than I do in our own churches.

> Continuation of Harvey's Letter in *The Brandon Times* p.81

Dinner Etiquette

After the church service of course it was dinner time and a good dinner I had. Roast duck, mashed potatoes, tomato salad, a tart for dessert and tea but not Russian. No one can make tea like the Russians. It takes long to get a meal served here in this country for it is the custom to spend a good deal of time eating. In America we see how fast we can eat, in vulgar terms, we gulp our food but here in Bulgaria we take a lot of time. This noon I spent one and a half hours and that is about minimum that any one is expected to spend. If you spend less time the waiters and hotel management want to ask you if you are not pleased with the food or the service. Any way the dinner was good.

Music

Dinner finished there were just ten minutes left to get to the opera. The opera is just across the park from the hotel and we reach it in less than five minutes. The opera I heard was "Mineon." I have heard the music in parts before but never the whole Opera. It was splendid. I was afraid that it would not be good for I hardly thought the Bulgarians were good musicians but they certainly sang well and acted like real artists. I haven't enjoyed an opera as much for a long time. I wish you might hear some good operas back home.

We Americans have spent so little time to developing our music that we have hardly anything we can call our own except Jazz.

Now I have just finished supper and am almost tired. Tomorrow I have a big hard job. It looks now that we will start the school in less than a month.

GETTING THE SCHOOL STARTED

Harvey's review of how the school came
into existence, written after his return to the U.S.

". . . The Y suggested a vocational school for 2-300 students between the ages 18 to 25. The government thought it a fine idea and offered to provide the buildings for the school if the Y.M.C.A. would accept 25 to 50 Bulgarian boys each term.

Discussion between Russian educators and engineers, and men well informed on the Russian character, concluded that the following courses would fit well into the demands of the conditions then existing in Bulgaria. In fact, there was need all over Europe for men trained in Surveying; Building and Architecture; and in Electro-Technical-Mechanical skills. Plans were then developed for such a vocational school, offering these three courses.

Mr. E.T. Colton asked me to be the Director and Dr. William Orr, retired Supt. of Schools, Springfield, Mass., Educational Director of the school. As County Agricultural Agent in Michigan my experience had been with practical education. Then during my years with the Y.M.C.A. in Siberia I had learned to speak the Russian language. We agreed that the school should be set up on a PROJECT BASIS, then Dr. Orr laid out the course plans accordingly."

Finding and Equipping Buildings

"My first task was to find suitable buildings as the government offerings were not satisfactory. Through a Bulgarian friend we found an old workshop of good size, and next to it, a building that had housed part of the Bulgarian Army.

To proceed . . . we conferred with the Berlin office of the Y.M.C.A. They agreed to our choice. Thus we leased sufficient space for an office, shops, classrooms and dormitory.

Mr. Nikelsky, a former General in the Russian Army, became the Director of the dormitory and dining room. To equip the rooms, our purchasing agent bought lumber, then the men in the Building course made frames for the beds on which they spread straw for mattresses. Meals were served in a dining room three blocks away at a cost of $.26 per student per day. The Russian Director and I often ate with the boys and found the food nourishing and tasty. This food and lodging was greatly appreciated by the students."

Finding Faculty

"To find the faculty I conferred with the Russian Red Cross whose director, Mr. Feldman, suggested Dr. Baranovski, a well-qualified educator, who was living in Bulgaria. These two men selected the Deans for the three courses: Mr. Glincetsky, Buildings; Mr. Harkotich, Electro-Technical-Mechanical; and Mr. Mironovitch, Surveying. These Deans were given responsibility to select their faculties. 24 members were chosen, graduates of Russian universities, and some experienced teachers. Others had worked in professional positions to qualify them as teachers."

Courses

"The minimum educational entrance requirement was completion of five grades of the Russian Gymnasium or its equivalent. The term was to be six months with no interruption. The school day was 8 hours—4 hours for lectures and 4 hours for practical work or shop itself.

The <u>Surveying Course</u> covered Algebra, Geometry, Trigonometry and Logarithms, Lettering, Mapping, the clear understanding of Surveying data and nomenclature. The students learned the actual use of all instruments used in taking data, the surveying of fields, and laying out water lines and cities. The aim was to train so thoroughly that the graduate could become an assistant to an official engineer . . .

The Electro-Technical-Mechanical Course covered the fields of tinsmithing, blacksmithing, locksmithing, electrical installations and repairs of all types of electrical appliances, the telephone and telegraph systems, installation and repair. The students were required, individually, to make bolts, chisels, hammers, calipers, and to do all kinds of welding, locksmith work to the exact degree of perfection so that bearings in machines could be set. In the electrical work, they had to understand motors, dynamos and install the same; wire and install the required switchboards for direct and alternating currents and do all repairs . . .

Staff of the School and Harvey (4th from left in first row)

The Building and Architectural Course covered the mathematics and drawing demanded for completing a structure from basement to ridge of the roof. Stone, brick and concrete work, plastering, interior decoration and painting were required. In the shop they learned the use of all carpenter's and cabinet maker's instruments and the actual making of doors, window frames, sash, stairways, framing roofs and all types of furniture."

Finances

"The sum of $50,000 was allotted to the school for buildings, equipment, faculty and office employees. The sum of several thousand dollars which exceeded the allotment was made up by order work done by the school in Bulgaria."

International Y.M.C.A. Committee

"The International Committee decided that in addition to the class work, the students should learn about the Y.M.C.A. so Mr. Arnold was sent to us. He found a house for clubwork and rest rooms adjoining one of the shops. Some boys enjoyed the freedom of these rooms and the program, but a majority were too busy studying . . . to become acquainted with the secretary in charge."

> The American Y.M.C.A. funded the vocational school in Bulgaria. Dr. Orr, as Educational Director, wrote letters about the progress of the school to Dr. John R. Mott, Y.M.C.A. National Office, 347 Madison Avenue, New York City.

STRUGGLES and SUCCESS

First Progress Report from Dr. Orr

"October 31, 1922
Dear Dr. Mott,

The story goes that soon after Woodrow Wilson left the sheltered life of a college president to enter on the stormy career of politics, that one of his friends asked him how he liked the change, and that the reply was somewhat as follows: The Scotchman in me says it might have been better to have stayed where I was, in peace and quiet, but the Irishman says "Just think what a lovely fight you are having every day of your life."

Our experiences in Bulgaria for the month past have made me thankful that there is a fair mixture of Irish blood (Ulster Brand) in my veins, for Harvey Smith and I have had an almost continuous struggle against the inertia, and in some cases, opposition of government officials. Athough as long ago as April, the Ministerial Council had approved the plan for a Vocational School for Russian Refugees and had virtually promised buildings for this purpose, action could not be secured. Even when a building was obtained by rental, various technicalities were raised by the Rooming Commission, as to our right to occupy although we had consulted all the sources of information at command and been assured the lease was entirely valid."

One Person Made a Difference

"Just when we were almost ready to abandon the struggle and the School, we met a graduate of Robert College, Minister Plenipotentiary of the King, in the office of Premier Stambuliski. This gentleman, Boris T. Kissimoff by name, asked us to tell him about the School, and at once grasped the significance of the enterprise and expressed his chagrin that we had been treated with so little consideration and fairness by government officials. The private secretary of Stambuliski also took up the cudgels vigorously in our behalf and other people of influence are also bestirring themselves. Yesterday we had assurances that our building would be free in a few days, so we confidently expect to see the School underway by the beginning of next week

One good result of the campaign we have conducted for the past month is that we have made the acquaintance of many people in the government and in private life who are alert to the possibilities in the school enterprise, and who will help in many ways in the future. We are told that Stambuliski is so impressed by the program of instruction that he wishes to enroll his son in one of the courses. Another by-product of no small moment is the attention that has been drawn to the Association and the potential constituency that has been secured as a basis for a vigorous forward movement for a modern Association in Bulgaria to enlist members of the Orthodox Churches as well as the Protestant Communions . . .

Now as to the School. It was a most agreeable and inspiring experience after the exasperating delays of the government and the tedious but all important work of organizing the machinery of the School, framing rules and regulations for students and faculty, devising forms, and outlining courses of instruction, to welcome the Constantinople delegation at the Station last Saturday afternoon."

Students Arrive

"There were 275 of these men, selected from 600 applications by Alexander at the Mayak. The train which brought the men from Varna was ahead of time and when we arrived they were already in the charge of Professor Baranovski, the Director of the School, who, with members of his faculty, was marshalling the refugees, in companies of about fifty each, for the march to the dormitory about two miles distant.

It was worthy of note that these men, who had been adrift for so many months, had so much hand luggage - an almost weird collection of bags, bundles, boxes, musical instruments, cooking utensils, bedding, and sets of chess and checkers. One of the party even had a dog, about which there was an animated discussion as the animal could not be allowed in the dormitory; at last one of the instructors took the pet into his own keeping."

Who Were These Students?

"One can easily understand that it was interesting to see this group, which epitomizes, as it were, the long agony of Russia, from the days of the Great War through the futile expeditions of Wrangel and Denikin against the Bolsheviks and the exodus from Odessa and the Crimea before the Red Terror. But the question might well be asked what there was to inspire one in such a motley crowd of men, in such desperate circumstances, clad in garments, that were for the most part mere apologies for clothing, and many of whom bore the marks of suffering and privation.

In the first place there was a manifest appreciation of the kindly interest that was being shown them; they had been living in tents at Varna under most trying conditions of weather, the journey by boat to Varna, and by train from Varna had been by no means comfortable and now that there was a prospect of better things their hopes were beginning to rise.

Again the Director of the School, Professor Baranovski, and his aides had organized the arrangements so effectively as to show that they had the capacity to direct and manage and this was a good augury for the school itself. There was a new light in the eyes of the men as they heard their own language from someone who spoke with authority and who was using that authority for their advantage. That five Americans, Mr. and Mrs. Links, from Stettin, here with supplies, Mr. Smith, Mr. Arnold, and Mr. and Mrs. Orr should come out on a cold, damp day to greet them in a strange city was an additional evidence of interest to give these forlorn people fresh courage and hope.

Then the new arrivals were young men, the average age 22, and in spite of the hardships they had experienced they were in good health and evidently had been carefully selected with regard to capacity and fitness for the tasks they were to undertake in the School. Finally, after our trying experiences with government officials, it was an agreeable surprise to see the excellent provisions made for the temporary housing and feeding of the men: of this more anon."

A Two Mile Walk to Beds, Blankets, Electricity and Food

"The belongings of the refugees were loaded into two large wagons and then we began our march through the streets of Sofia none too clean at any time, and now wet and miry. Although there were many people about, as the hour was near six o'clock, the small procession attracted but little attention despite the odd appearance of many of the Russians. The pace was a brisk one and two miles to the dormitory were covered in half an hour.

Naturally the refugees were curious as to the provisions made for them and as they neared the imposing pile of buildings which make up the Army School - the West Point of Bulgaria - there were manifest signs of wonderment and even of doubt as to whether these were their quarters. Then when they saw the dormitories provided with clean bedding sheets and blankets, and more than that, pillows, the rooms with electric light and heated, the dining room with its good food and neat tables, used also by the cadets, it must have seemed to many of them after the tents of Varna and the even worse experiences at Constantinople and Gallipoli, as a veritable paradise. I am glad to make acknowledgment to the Bulgarian government for this deed of hospitality.

The Georgi Rakowski Military Academy (West Point of Bulgaria)

Since their arrival the papers of the men have been carefully scrutinized and several of the group have been rejected for failure to comply with the regulations and conditions of admission. It is our purpose to put the School on a thoroughly sound basis and to secure a homogeneous student body, as to carry along those who are not willing or who have limitations, either mental or physical, would put too great a burden on the teaching staff."

Getting Buildings Ready to Start the School

"Meanwhile the buildings are being cleared of the tenants in occupation and thoroughly fumigated. The plant of the School consists of a hotel with fifty two rooms, a shop equipped with power and some heavy lathes for the electrical courses, a dwelling house to supplement the hotel for rooming purposes, while the regular classwork in theoretical subjects will be given in a nearby Gymnasium, the Principal of which is showing a most helpful spirit . . . we are fortunate in securing such an equipment situation as it is in the central part of Sofia, in a neighborhood where the students can secure practical experience in actual employment on building and electrical installation. The distance to the suburbs is not great so that the men in Surveying can easily reach open spaces for their practice work."

A New Approach to Education

"As you will see the School is intended to emphasize the practical side and a close relation is to be maintained between the theoretical work and the jobs in the shop and in the field. Professor Baranovski, as a trained engineer, is enthusiastic over this phase of the enterprise and has already had a number of meetings with his faculty to discuss methods and topics. Some of the educational people in Bulgaria are watching the School with great interest, as this type of vocational training has not been developed in this country, which is in great need of such schools. We are hoping to make a demonstration that will have a good influence on their educational system.

The intention is furthermore to send the students in relays, as soon as possible, to secure experience in actual wage earning and thus secure a revenue for the School. It has been found that such a procedure is an advantage from the educational as well as from the financial standpoint."

Political Situation: Value of the School

"The Greek debacle in Asia Minor and the impending changes in Constantinople and Thrace have resulted in a new inrush of fugitives from those parts, as the impression grows that the Kemalites are determined to drive out all Christians. At present the only country that seems willing or able to make any provision at all for Russians is Bulgaria and her resources are being taxed to the utmost. So it may be that a school like ours, which will give a practical training and fit these unfortunates to become wage earners and thus contribute to the economic resources of the country, may be the means of helping to solve a most pressing and desperate problem likely to grow more intense as the full effects of the transfer of territory to the Turks are felt . . ."

Thinking Ahead: a Model for Russia in the Future

"Apart from the immediate value of the School, I am impressed with its relations to any future work of the Association in Russia itself. As you will see from the memorandum sent you under separate cover a careful record is being kept of the several steps in the organization and equipment of the School and this material will constitute an excellent guide in case the Association should undertake educational work in Russia.

It may be taken for granted that such vocational training will be one of the greatest factors in putting Russia on her feet again. Copies of this material are filed in Berlin and New York and a third copy is kept in our files. In like manner all the material of instruction is being carefully preserved so that there will be at command teacher manuals and texts.

Among the staff and student body there are men whose addresses will be kept as they are likely to be valuable aids to our own secretaries in their work in Russia in the future. It is planned to develop in connection with the School an Association program so that the men will become familiar with our methods and be imbued with the right spirit. Professor Baranovski is a man who would be invaluable in any educational work we may do in the future, here or elsewhere.

Harvey Smith and the School

I wish also to speak of Harvey G. Smith the head of the School. Smith saw service in Siberia in the critical days of the Kolchak movement and from what I have learned won his spurs by heroic efforts. In his management of the school he has had to contend against the impossible and has shown business and diplomatic capacity under most trying conditions.

He has a good understanding of the Russians and likes that people. He has dealt with some of the obstructionists in the government here, without gloves, and still keeps their good will. He is bent on making the school the largest kind of a success and hopes that it may in some way prove an open door to Russia.

This letter was begun over a week ago as another crisis in the School affairs developed and I had for a time to give all my attention to interviews with officials . . . Sofia is a good place for residence and Mrs. Orr and I are keeping very well. We have good news from the children and the grandchildren (5) and so are content to remain on this side longer. It is indeed a great privilege to do something to bring in the better day of righteousness.

Occasionally I find relaxation by trying my hand at a bit of verse and hope you will pardon me for including two specimens, growing out of Bulgarian experiences.

    Cordially yours,
      William Orr"

THE SCHOOL OPENS
Second Progress Report from Dr. Orr

"November 19, 1922
Dear Dr. Mott:

Events of the greatest significance are now coming thick and fast in Bulgaria . . .

May I say, in the first place, that we are now in full possession of the buildings for the School and also that, for the past two weeks, the students have been occupied with preliminary work, as making bed frames, cleaning rooms, and erecting a blacksmith shop to supplement the factory. We are also in a fair way to secure a garage . . . that will complete our equipment for shops.

The school will open next Wednesday, and a week from today, Sunday the 26th, comes the formal opening and the blessing of the buildings by an Orthodox priest.

We attribute the change in the attitude of the government to the personal efforts of King Boris, who gave Mr. Smith and me an audience of nearly an hour last week and, who, after he had heard about the School, expressed his approval of the enterprise and said he would speak to the Ministry in charge of buildings. Certainly within the past few days we have had the most cordial support.

Boris III King of Bulgaria 1894-1943

But even more significant are the developments that have marked the Week of Prayer. Through Mr. Alexieff, the National Y.M.C.A. Secretary for Bulgaria, Metropolitan Stephan was enlisted in the arrangements for a meeting for students, to be on a broad religious basis.

Then, through our own Mr. Arnold, a special service was held for the students of the school who are still housed at the Army School about a mile out of the city. This service was conducted by a Russian bishop, who expressed his satisfaction in being able to meet the men. Mr. Arnold tells us that the students were most grateful, as for many of them it was the first service of this kind in years. A week ago there was a service in the rooms of the Bulgarian Y.M.C.A. (Evangelical) addressed by a prominent member of the Bulgarian Orthodox Church . . . This afternoon comes a special service for students at the Russian church.

The meeting arranged by Mr. Alexieff . . . was held in the National Cathedral and brought together members of the leading religious bodies, both Evangelical and Orthodox, in a way that as near as I can learn has never been the case before in Bulgaria. The Metropolitan Stephan conducted the service and made an address at its conclusion. Mr. Smith who has a fair command of Bulgarian tells me that the speaker made frequent references to the Y.M.C.A. and in praise of that agency.

At the close of the service the Metropolitan held an informal reception and greeted representatives of the Y.M.C.A. and Y.W.C.A. in a most cordial manner and repeated his belief in those organizations. Mr. Smith thanked the Metropolitan on behalf of the International Committee and Mr. Alexieff expressed appreciation of the Bulgarian Association . . .

The service itself was a very impressive one and devoid of the formality which one sometimes finds connected with ritual. This quality of sincerity and simplicity was in large measure due to the fine spiritual level set by the Metropolitan in his prayers and sermon. He is indeed a man of broad sympathies and one who radiates the truth and life of the gospel . . .

There was a good attendance of students from our own school and from the university and I could see that they were much impressed by the talk and the service as well as by the personality of the Metropolitan.

St. Alexander Nevski Cathedral - Eastern Orthodox Christianity Designed by Russian architect Pomerantsev, 1912. The gold plated dome is 148' and Russian and Bulgarian artists created icons and frescoes.

It was a notable and significant occasion in that there came together for common worship members of the Protestant (Evangelical) group, of the Bulgarian Orthodox Church and of the Russian Orthodox Church.

We hope this is a symbol of a gradual evolution of the Association in Bulgaria from its present restricted character including only Protestants - to a movement embracing members of the Orthodox communions . . .

                    William Orr"

STUDENTS IN THE CLASSROOM

"From daylight till dark they were at work. At first the tasks were simple, learning to use hammer and forge - "cutting white heated iron." Project No. 10 was "joining separate pieces of covering iron by oblique or angular joint." Project No. 20 was "plan and estimate of the electric light fitting and equipment in the basement of the Dormitory building of the Vocational School." In the Building Trade section, 100 men, Project No. 12 was "construction of a table, joiner's work." In Surveying, 100 men, Project No. 4. "construction of a cross scale with a given preciseness."

"One day Prime Minister Stambuliski . . . dropped in for inspection. Picking up a bench tool and noting its quality, he asked what factory had produced it. "That was made by a student, Your Excellency," said the instructor. 'Impossible,' said the Premier."

—*Projectitis* p. 75

STUDENTS LEARN ON THE JOB

Harvey's course descriptions.

Surveying Course

"The government requested the men to lay out a survey for a new water line from the Rilo Mountains, 50 miles distant, to supply additional water to Sofia. This accomplishment delivered to the city the complete figures and maps of the entire distance."

Electro-Technical-Mechanical Course

"For practical application of their knowledge they did motor winding and installed special switches in the dormitory which saved the school expense. They also did outside jobs for Bulgarian friends."

Building Course

"The Bulgarian Secretary of Foreign Affairs asked if the school would be able to build him a house if he furnished all the materials. This they did, making it of brick and stone and covering the roof with clay tile. When finished, the Secretary invited all the Deans, Dr. Baranovski and me to a dinner in his new home."

STUDENT LIFE AT THE SCHOOL

"Some days later King Boris appeared to look over this novel institution, and went away highly pleased. Other visitors, such as the American Minister, the Allied Control officers, and Karsavina, the Russian dancer, came evenings for musical entertainments, for these students were men of quality, doing Tchaikovsky and Grieg no less creditably than they made hand forged tools . . ."
—*Projectitis* p.75

The students composed a school song and created a school choir and orchestra, both of which were part of the 1924 commencement ceremony. An Orthodox priest provided Sunday afternoon messages which were attended by 90% of the students.

The School Soccer team

KING BORIS and THE SCHOOL

It was very important for the school to have the support of the King, so Harvey must have been very pleased to receive this letter in the 4th month of the school's existence.

> Cabinet de Sa Majesté le Roi des Bulgares.
>
> Sofia, le 18. février 1923.
>
> Monsieur H. J. Smith,
> représentant du Comité International de
> l'American Y. M. C. A.,
> En Ville.
>
> Monsieur,
>
> J'ai l'avantage de vous accuser réception en haut lieu de votre aimable missive du 9. de ce mois. Sa Majesté le Roi, mon Auguste Maître, fut vivement touché par cette aimable attention de votre part et me chargea de vous exprimer Sa sincère gratitude.
>
> Agréez, Monsieur, l'assurance de ma parfaite considération.
>
> Le Secrétaire
> D. Mihoff

Cabinet of His Majesty the King of the Bulgars
Sofia, February 23, 1923

Mr. H. G. Smith, representative of the International Committee of the American Y.M.C.A.

I have the favor of acknowledging, at the highest level, having received your letter this very month. His Majesty the King, my august Master, was vividly touched by your friendly attentiveness and charged me with expressing His sincere gratitude.

Please, Sir, be assured of my complete consideration.
The Secretary (with signature)

COMMENCEMENT for FIRST CLASS
April 1923

"It was a severe test for all factors, students, faculty, administration and method, and it is to the credit of all that six months after the start 273 men completed with certificates of competence, and within four days every man had a job, eighty percent of them on the line of work studied. Before, they had been useless refugees in penury and hopelessness; after six months' training, the average immediate wage was $2 a day, jobs varying from carpenters to shop foremen . . .

It was a venture . . . this Projectitis in Bulgaria, and it hangs on. The School is still running, with a new lot of three hundred students . . ."
—*Projectitis* p.75

SUMMER SCHOOL 1923

A night school was conducted for about 150 men.

Fond du Lac Man Teaches Men to Live; Heads Unique School At Sofia, Bulgaria

Harvey G. Smith Heping Refugees Left in Destitution

Reports received here from the International Committee of the Y. M. C. A. reveal the unique character and the success of work being carried on in Sofia, Bulgaria, by Harvey G. Smith, formerly of Oakfield and Brandon. He will be remembered as having returned less than two years ago from long service under the American Y. M. C. A. in Siberia. In July, 1922, he accepted an invitation from the International Committee to organize and direct a trade school for Russian refugees in the Bulgarian capital.

At the end of the first term of the school, established by Mr. Smith, diplomas were awarded to 273 men for work satisfactorily completed. There were more than 300 men in various courses during the term. The studies comprise three branches, surveying, building trades and electro- technique.

The school is one of the means used by the Y. M. C. A. to help the thousands of refugees left in destitution as well as exile by the war. Its purpose is to train skilled workmen at a time when they are greatly needed.

In a speech which he delivered at the commencement of the vocational school the president of the Students' Council said of this experiment attempted under the leadership of Mr. Smith:

"Normal connection of theory and practice, with preponderancy to the latter has given a splendid result. Theory has made it possible to turn the dream of many of us about universities into real life. Practical training has made us fit for useful and productive work. We feel strong now and know what we are worth as men of work. That is our great privilege. Each one knows what he is able to do and how he can use his forces for securing life and improving in the trades which shall be one day so useful to our country—If God grants that the slavery chains fall down from our beloved motherland, we shall return then to our homes to participate in the work of restoration with all the knowledge and experience we have gained here."

In speaking of the difficulties with which both the faculty and the students had to struggle, one of the professors told of the necessity for the creation of working apparatus on the spot. The instructors and teachers wrote, during the course of the six-months term, twenty-one handbooks and prepared over 200 projects of practical exercises.

The reports indicate that great interest is felt in the school by both church and government. Indeed, the undertaking, they point out, could never have been consummated had it not been for the sympathetic interest of the Bulgarian government. One of the features of this work is the bringing together in one school of the adherents to the three churches, the Russian, the Orthodox and the Protestant.

At the closing exercises Mr. Smith spoke of the new conception of education and the part it played in the ideals and program of the school.

"From the early hours of morning until the late hours of night every man was at his task," he said. "And for what purpose? I believe I can honestly say not to educate as was once the common idea in education, but to prepare men to live. Education for life has been our motto."

Mr. Smith is now organizing the work for the school's second year.

In a Fond du Lac newspaper: Harvey was not a "Fond du Lac Man" but lived in the nearby small town of Brandon, Wisconsin.

Note last sentence of article: "Mr. Smith is now organizing the work for the school's second year."

Faculty Write Texts for Their Classes

> This order was for texts to be published to begin the second year 1923-24. The faculty had created these texts and manuals, with illustrations, during the first year of the school.

```
Mr. H. G. Smith                                August 7, 1923
14 Isker Street
Sofia - Bulgaria.

My dear Smith:

       On Saturday I telegraphed you that we are prepared to
undertake the publication of the texts prepared in the Vocational
School in Sofia.  In this letter I desire to recapitulate the
several important points in this connection.

       I.   Our agreement to publish concerns the following books:
```

		No. of Sheets	APPROXIMATELY Cuts Sq. Cm.	Order
I.				
1.	Review Course in Mathematics			
	1. Algebra	7-8	6000-7000	1
	2. Geometry			
	3. Trigonometry			
2.	Technology of Materials			
	1. Materials			
	2. Working with materials	5-6	5000	2
3.	Physics	5-6	5000	6
4.	Chemistry	2	500	5
5.	Machine Parts	5-6	9000	8
6.	Electricity & Magnetism	5-6	4000	4
7.	Theory of Building Construction	15-16	18000-20000	3
8.	Architecture (Construction)	8-9	14000-16000	7
9.	Practical Manual of Projects	30	20000-25000	

```
       1- Planing
       2- Carpentry
       3- Masonry
       4- Stucco Work
       5- Blacksmithing
       6- Locksmith
       7- Tinsmith
       8-Electro Technics
```

Three additional pages listed further details from the YMCA press. Signed by Paul B. Anderson

INTERLUDE in the RILO MOUNTAINS

Rilo Mountains - Bulgarian artist

"September 9, 1923
Dear Folks,
    There seems to be a long lapse of time since I last wrote you. . . . Just what we have done during these last few weeks we better record in a letter and so this cool, quiet Sunday afternoon I am taking a few reminiscences of the past days and hope thereby to bring you into the present of my life here in Bulgaria.

My days here in Sofia became so tiresome and tedious that I felt that something should be done. I could not take time for a long vacation and yet I knew that what I needed more than anything else was a rest. For a number of years I have not known a real feeling of lightness and freeness that ought to come to me as the days go along. Thus one bright afternoon with my bedding roll filled with the normal comforts of life, such as bathrobes, bedroom slippers, shaving outfits, sweaters, wool shirts and shoes, I started for Teham Korea.

Teham Korea is a summer resort in the Rilo Mountains of Bulgaria which are the highest in the Balkan peninsula, approximately ten thousand feet. The way to this home in the pine forests is not as you would expect - railroad - but by autobus over a beautiful winding road along one of the swift rivers of the country, the water of which furnishes part of the city of Sofia with electricity. I did not think much of this latter idea as I rode along into the heights of the mountains. I had seen so much of the city and people that I let my mind wander over the things that made the river and not what the water of that age long river could make for people.

The chasm through which the river and the road pass is most gorgeous in these days. The green is still in its high color and in amongst it the signs of the on coming season are visible, the bright colors of autumn.

But with the best of beauty at one's command every minute, the ride became a little tiresome, at least for weary bones like mine and I was glad that finally on the hour of eight our lumbering old grey bus arrived and all the passengers met by friends or left alone went their various ways.

I had sent for a room reservation but for some reason my letter failed to arrive and thus no room was available. However, I had some friends that I had learned to know during the year, and so I finally found a room and a bed and there I stayed during my ten days in the mountains. It is always good to have friends and these folks who are Bulgarians were as good to me as if I had been at home.

The mountains here were glorious. From almost everywhere one could see the highest peaks beckoning one to the tops. Each day I walked miles and when night came after a day's traveling I was so tired that sleep came as it used to when out on the farm. It was "Early to bed and early to rise." There are never many people in these mountains because they are so large. The slopes and valleys are covered with endless forests of pine, spruce and balsam with now and then a beech and birch. The mountain peaks are almost above the vegetation line. No trees grow on them and the last of real trees are at about seven thousand feet.

View of Rilo Mountains and Lakes

At the bottom of the valleys, brooks sing their songs in minors and majors and some only babble and rush. One day in my wanderings, I sat beside one that had traveled a long way down the mountains and seemed more than glorious as it gushed by me. As I sat there I could hear it talk in a deep low voice, but never was

I able to understand the brook's language, but it was most soothing and quieting and seemed to make me feel the life and newness of nature. One day it looked so good I jumped in and had an icy bath. Oh, and it was good. My skin filled with deep pink color as that old brook gurgled and babbled on its endless journey while it was making me happy. Those were great days with the brooks and the trees, the valleys and the mountains.

The highest peak of all the Balkans is Musalla, a Turkish word meaning pray to Allah. It defies most people all their lives but to me it was a stimulation. I had wanted to climb something high all these years and never found or had time to do my climbing. When I was a kid at home there were no mountains although the Ledge (a small, glacial ridge in Wisconsin) looked as if it were, before my reasoning and stature had come to its present state.

One day after considerable planning and working, a party of friends, six in all with a horse to carry the blankets to the camping ground at the first lake, started up the valley to the mountain that had defied us for more than a week. We started at eleven o'clock in the morning, stopped for lunch at about one and at four-thirty were in camp, a large rock alongside of which we built a fire that we kept going from the time of our arrival to our departure.

It was a job to find wood and there in the bleakness of that old valley almost above the tree line the wind blew its blast of cold that made us shiver. We had our supper, laid out our blankets and rolled up for the night which gave hardly anyone more than an hour of sleep. In the darkness of the morning we made tea, ate an egg with a slice of bread and then slowly in the darkness and with staff in hand, made our way to the trail that takes one to the top.

In the glowing dawn it was a glorious sight to walk up and up past the hidden lakes, the last year's snow, until at last the top was scaled in the rising sun. Where the air is light and the climbing heavy, one's muscles and whole body almost refuse to go on at times. The icy cold wind which seemed as if it had been sent by winter almost froze one even though the sun glowed through the frost and the mists in the valleys and on the horizon. It was a great feeling to be up there and almost sad to come down.

Musalla is the highest peak - 9596' - in Bulgaria.
Its name is interpreted as "near God" or "place for prayer."

In about half an hour we started back, glad that we had come but cold as the blowing winds. The descent was easier than the ascent. Back to camp we had breakfast and then packed and came down the beautiful valley in the morning hot sun, hot and thirsty and hungry for dinner. It was two o'clock when we arrived and the journey finished. I shall always remember my first mountain climb - it seemed like a look into the world, something I had never seen before.

My first ten days of tramping ended and feasting as well, for my friends would not let me go to the restaurant as I thought I ought. There was cream with berries every morning and all the milk that I could drink. I certainly have gained and I feel much, much better. Bulgaria has been good to me in these days. These Bulgarian friends are almost American, the children have finished the American College at Constantinople and one of the girls has been in the U.S. for three years doing work with the Y.W.C.A.. She was Student Secretary at the University of Minnesota for one year. The whole family is very brilliant and talented.

After a few days back in Sofia I returned again to the mountains to spend Labor Day and walk and rest in preparation for the heavy year ahead.

Now I am back here and already have done a good deal of work in preparation for the new year in the school. The government has been most cordial during the past week. For a long time I thought I would have some difficulties but now it looks as if the full assistance possible by the government would be given. It will save me from lots of worry.

The weather has been very dry, not a drop of rain for several months. The harvests are over. Fruit, apples, grapes and watermelons are on the market in large quantities. The dust is terrible . . .

        Always,
          Harvey"

COMMENCEMENT   APRIL 1924

1. Prayer
    Clergy of Russian Orthodox Church
2. The Progress of the School
    Professor Baranovski
3. The Meaning of the Vocational School to the Students
    Mr. Mumrikoff, Student Representative
4. Cooperation & Friendship in Bulgaria
    Mr. Radoslavoff, Chief Secretary of the
    Bulgarian Ministry of Education
5. Charge to the Students of the Vocational School
    Mr. Harvey Smith
6. Presentation of Diplomas
    Mr. Charles Wilson, American Minister to
    Bulgaria
7. Concert
    Vocational School Choir and Orchestra
8. Announcements and Tea

Professor Baranovski

"Ladies and Gentlemen:

300 men were accepted to the second six months' course of the American YMCA Vocational School: 100 to every division. 15 left, owing to different reasons, six did not receive Diplomas. 279 students graduated from the school - from the Electro-Technical Division - 93, from the Building Division – 94, and from the Surveying Division - 92 . . .

The popularity of the school gave us many orders from outside and we were able to make our program larger. Finally the work capacity of the students was of a very high standing.

Only 8% not attending the lectures; 4% being on service; 3% owing to illnesses and only 1% without sufficient reasons. With this course the YMCA may finish its activity in Sofia.

During the whole period of the school's existence $56,000 were spent which makes about 8,000,000 Levas. 700 students graduated from the school.

Besides the material help, the idea of a short practical education was demonstrated for the first time with a very great success . . .

The whole organization was done under the direction of our deeply respected Mr. Smith, for whom everyone of us has the profoundest gratitude and affection.

I also express my gratitude to the faculty . . .

My best wishes to the students and my heartiest thanks to them for their honest and serious work."

Mr. Mumrikoff, Student Representative

"Our dear Mr. Smith, Dear Director and Instructors,

Saying goodbye to you, I must express the feelings of which our hearts are full and to tell you what is the real meaning of the American YMCA vocational school for everyone of us.

When six months ago, we came here, we had no idea about this school, and it was soon evident that during the short period of the course, we should get even more knowledge than we ever expected. We saw what a hard work you had to do in giving us all that was possible, and we greatly appreciate your care which surrounded us at every step in our daily life.

During these six months, not only did we get the theoretical and practical knowledge, but we also developed ourselves physically and spiritually.

We believe that the time spent in the school is a bright spot in our wandering abroad and we shall never forget it. We leave the school quite ready for the work we have chosen as our profession.

Mr. Smith, you, the friend of the Russian youth, led a hard fight for the existence of our school. We could not fail to see that you gave your entire self to the continual care of the students.

Will you bring to the American YMCA and all of your countrymen our heartiest Russian "Spassibo" for the great deed that is done here."

Mr. Radoslavoff, Chief Secretary of The Bulgarian Ministry of Public Education

"I am happy that I have the honor to be present to this lovely celebration as a Representative of the Bulgarian government. The success achieved by these courses is obvious and doubtless.

Through the well organized and skillful teaching of the theoretical and practical knowledge, many young men, Russian and Bulgarian, have learned in such a short time a profession, which will give them the possibility to earn their living in an honest way and to work for their own welfare, as well as for the good of others . . .

And you, dear students, I congratulate you in successfully finishing these courses. I wish you good health and useful work."

Charge to the Students - Mr. Smith

"Today we have met together for the purpose of giving official recognition to the closing of the second six months' course of the Vocational School in Sofia, Bulgaria, and of presenting to you students your Diplomas, which you have so diligently earned as a result of your study during the past six months . . .

Students, both Bulgarian and Russian, six months ago, you came to this school without a vocation, you were untrained in any profession, your morale was at a low ebb, it was as if you had lost hope. Now, as I look into your faces and as I have seen you these six months just now closing, I see there an eager eye, a force, a purpose which I believe will take you in and through all your years into a state of achievement, results, and not least, happiness which is what all men seek.

Your friends, the American people through the American Y.M.C.A. established this school that these results might be obtained. They believe that you are now ready to join the great achieving people in working for yourself, for your progress and for society. The great request of your friends is that you not disappoint them . . .

You students of the Surveying course join on the morrow that great and honorable company that has conquered the pathless wilderness and directed the development of the people throughout the world. Go to them and add your honest effort to that which has already been accomplished.

You students of the Electro-Technical and Mechanical course join a worthy fellowship also, the great family of moulders of iron and brass, copper and silver and the directors of that electrical current which is yet to bring revolution upon revolution into industry and way of life. Go forth to your enviable task.

And you students of the course in Building and Architecture, join the workers of wood and stone. You have an honorable record. Your predecessors in antiquity raised those mighty Pyramids which still call forth the wonders of men. Your fellow workers are today building the skyscrapers of this modern age. It is for you to go forth to build homes, factories and markets and perhaps to raise temples to God.

You students of all the courses are copartners with the Great Workman God Himself who wearies not in his task of continuous creation.

I congratulate you in your success at this school. Your American friends rejoice with you in your achievements and expect you to show yourselves worthy of their trust. Your Bulgarian friends are ready to receive you. And you, my dear Russian friends, will some day be welcomed to your native land where you will build the Great Russia that is yet unknown. Go forth into the world and achieve and live a full life."

Mr. Wilson, American Minister to Bulgaria
"Students of the American Vocational School:

Your Director has done me the honor of asking me to hand you today the diplomas awarded to you on your completion of the present course, and I have accepted with great pleasure . . .

This School, unique in its kind in Bulgaria, is very well appreciated on the part of the Bulgarian Government, and I am authorized to say that the Government will do everything on its part to help out in order that the school be retained and continue its existence in Bulgaria . . .

And, you, dear students, I congratulate you in successfully finishing these courses. I wish you good health and useful work."

COMMENCEMENT and FUTURE FUNDING

Mr. E. T. Colton (World Service Y.M.C.A. Secretary)
8 Kochstrasse, Berlin

"Dear Mr. Colton:

I am enclosing a complete copy of the program and addresses given at our commencement on April 28.

This day was a most remarkable one in that the school showed its greatest achievement during the period of its existence. Over 120 guests representing Bulgarians, British and Americans were present for Commencement.

In order that we could give a more complete understanding of the work of the courses, each division prepared an exhibit of the work done during the six months. Thus there was an exhibit of the practical and theoretical work including printed books and lectures of the Surveying course, Building and Architecture and Electro-Technical and Mechanical. I will send you pictures later.

All of the visitors were most unanimous in their praises of the work of the school. There was not a single objection raised even by our Bulgarian friends, thus we can conclude so far as the accomplishments of the school are concerned, that the courses give most remarkable and valuable results and are desired here in Bulgaria . . .

By the time you receive this letter we will know your last word relative to the school. For the sake of the school my hope is that sufficient funds are available to continue at least one more year.

                Yours truly,
                Harvey Smith"

GRADUATES EXPRESS THANKS
Excerpts from letters

To Professor Baranovski

"The first thing I want to tell you, that I bring to you and all our Faculty my sincerest thanks for what they have taught me and with what they made me acquainted. Without this knowledge I should remain here as in Bulgaria an ordinary workman. But the certificate you gave me helped me a great deal as well as your letters of recommendation. What concerns the certificate, I must tell you sincerely that it produces a magic affect about the administration of the factory and the foremen.

I work now as joiner and receive Frs.3 per hour - such a sum could never be earned in Bulgaria, and I live now quite comfortably. I have a good furnished room for two, which cost comparatively Frs. 50 per month for each of us. I ask you again to transmit my gratitude to everybody in the school."

A. Beyer to the Dormitory Steward

"There are several days since I received quite an independent work of planning the village Khlevene, Lovetch district.

The work is very minute; I have to work not less than 12 hours per day. Room and board from the Community. The relations with the peasants are excellent. I spend my money for the most soldier-like needs: washing, soap and tobacco - thus my month's salary Leva I. 200, remains untouched. If nothing will hinder, I expect to finish the work in this village and to continue the work in the next one."

S. Neklioukoff to the Dormitory Steward

"Remembering your quite exceptionally kind attention towards me, I resolve to write you how I feel in the place of new service . . . Our chiefs appreciated from the first our skill and there are already several days that we all, who received employment through the Ministry of Agriculture, are appointed to independent work.

We make surveying in the woods on the Rodop Balkans. The air in the pine forest is fresh, the scenery is beautiful, which transforms our work in a pleasant excursion.

As for the wages our expectations did not fulfill in the full measure. Our travelling expenses were not reimbursed, thus our salary becomes twice less than we were told when we were engaged. We cannot complain however from the financial point of view, as owing to the boarding by groups, the living expenses are very small. It will be possible to save Leva 1.000. monthly . . ."

Mr. Petroff to the Dormitory Steward

". . . I am working at the factory of Andre Citroyen, have a good position and what is most important, work in my specialty, the painting. I receive 25 Frcs per day. All of our students have a quite satisfactory service in different factories. Our certificates are of great value here. I am very glad I came to Paris . . ."

To Mr. Smith

". . . About a month and a half, I received an employment in the Ministry of Agriculture and I am working since in the forest-surveying party. My work has a special surveying character, my duties covering quite independent theodolite surveying. I can positively say now that I have a profession, giving the means to have an interesting and well payed work.

. . . I have the pleasure to testify that our chiefs believe that during the six months we got a maximum of knowledge and practical training. Allow me to express you my deepest respect and gratefulness."

A group of Students and Faculty of the school.
Harvey (in center above 1st row)

DINNER HONORING HARVEY

> Harvey had indicated he might leave at the end of this school year, thus references were made to his comments in a few of the speeches.
>
> All speeches/excerpts are dated May 10, 1924.

A Student

"Dear Mr. Smith,

It is always a great happiness to me to greet you, and today I am especially happy, because I can do it in this large friendly and unanimous family.

The day of our commencement, April 28, you gave to all of us a very flattering attestation - today you have to listen how you will be attested by us.

Every refugee, every emigrant encounters on his way many foreigners, and we must consider ourselves exceptionally happy that in our emigrants' way we met just you - and the reason is as follows:

When the foreigners meet each other, they often do not understand each other - their national features seem sometimes funny and quite uncomprehensible. You, Mr. Smith, although you spent a very short time in Russia, and in the Far East, during the hard time of the Civil War - you know well the character and the psychology of the Russians - thus you always understand us. During our emigration the foreigners never trusted us, but you, when organizing the big and difficult work at Sofia, proved to us credit since the first day of our work together. Finally your endless and steady altruism, your life devoted to the cultural development of the humanity and your unweariness, were for us continual example of life. Even in the moment when you were displeased with somebody, you never forgot, and always thought of the good of this man . . .

These three particular features of your personality Mr. Smith - your understanding of the Russians, your trust in us, and your endless altruism, were the main basis, which gathered us here in your honor, like a good family, and we come to greet you with love, dear Mr. Smith. There is no doubt that your high moral qualities were the reason why our school reached such exceptional success.

Addressing myself in conclusion to all members of our party, I must add some sad words to our joyful speeches. In a private conversation Mr. Smith told me about his almost final decision to return during the summer to America, independent of the continuation of the school or no. It is impossible to imagine at once our school without Mr. Smith. I tried to convince Mr. Smith not to leave our school, I gave him all the proofs that I could imagine, but it seems to me that I could not fluctuate him in his decision.

Thus I ask you all to entreat and to convince Mr. Smith not to leave us alone. Maybe where I alone failed, you all will be more successful

In my peroration, dear Mr. Smith, accept my greetings and the deepest gratitude from all my heart for all what you have done to the Russian refugees."

Mr. Pintchoukoff, Dean of the Surveying Division

"Mr. Pintchoukoff greets Mr. Smith in the name of the Surveying Division and expresses his gratitude for the kindness and care, which Mr. Smith always proved to the Faculty of the Division.

The Russian emigrants have met many nations during their wandering away from the native land, and only the Americans, Mr. Smith in particular, showed a real feeling and helping them, and we all who have been in touch with Mr. Smith can only express the deep appreciation of such care. Our school song, written by one of the students, says all what we think about the school and how we love it. It also speaks about the great meaning which the school has for the future Russia.

We shall never forget the Vocational School in Sofia working under the skillful Direction of Mr. Smith."

A Student

"Dear Mr. Smith,

It is a great privilege for me to take part on such a lovely feast, organized in honour of you . . . All of us, who are present here, are close witnesses, during the last two years, of an immense energy and a wonderful skill shown by Mr. Smith for the organization of these courses and the shops to them. Hard was the task but the choice was one of the most successful - Mr. Smith was the best fitted for the performing of this great work. As a worthy collaborator to Mr. Smith in this hard and great work the Providence has sent our most respected Director, Mr. Baranovski, who took up a great part of the burden of Mr. Smith. They both dedicated themselves entirely for the organization of the courses for the theoretical, practical, physical, moral and religious education of the students.

Many obstacles were broken, many difficulties surmounted. It was necessary for one to have a will of steel and a constant watchfulness to attain those results, for which, all of us here are witnesses . . .

In these courses was not only given a profession, but something more valuable . . . characters were formed and ennobled wills were strengthened; souls were winged; hearts were encouraged and men were prepared for any kind of noble work . . . All these students will be the pioneers on the field of the productive work - physical, moral and spiritual, wherever the Providence will send them and wherever they may go, they will carry in their hearts the gratitudes to those who gave them such valuable attributes . . .

The American YMCA supplied the financial support for organizing these courses, but our most respected Mr. Smith and Mr. Baranovski gave their best and most valuable they had - they gave their souls and hearts to these courses . . .

With his skillful direction, with his keen spirit of observation, with his untired working, with his arrangements, always given in time, with his generosity and patience, with his cheerfulness and kindness, with his willingness to help and encourage everybody, Mr. Smith is an example worthy of following. These attributes are highly appreciated by everyone who has been in touch with Mr. Smith . . .

Dear Mr. Smith, we heartily wish you that God grant you life, energy and courage to continue for long years the work for the good of the young men all over the world.   Christ has risen!"

Dean of the Building Division

"Dear Mr. Smith,

I am very sorry that illness deprives me of the pleasure to pass several hours in your company at our modest meal.

. . . Let us hope that if in the future God will grant to continue our work it will be only with you, dear Mr. Smith, for whose health I lift in my thoughts the goblet and join in the cheers my friends who are with you . . .

Hourrah and Spassibo!"

THE BENCH
A Gift to Harvey from the Students

This walnut bench, with its detailed carvings in the wood, was a gift to Harvey from students in the school. It was built so it could be disassembled in four parts for shipping, which is how Harvey was able to bring it back to the U.S. in 1924.

Length 57"
Width 13"
Height 19"
Thickness 2.5"

The carving is on all four sides of the bench as well as on the legs at each end.

It is impressive to think of the time the students spent in creating and then carving these designs.

The Dormitory Steward
"Our dear and deeply respected Mr. Smith,

Allow me to bring you once more the most hearty greetings from all the students of the school.

I receive many letters from the students of the last year's course and I spoke with all those who have just finished and just left our Dormitory. They all without exception are deeply touched and do not forget the warmth and the gentleness which they felt in you as soon as they were admitted to the school and during all the time of the course.

From all points of Bulgaria, tired, exhausted and insulted they gathered under the roof of the school, where they met your attention, friendliness, comfort and untiring care.

They found your soul so kindred to them, understanding better our Russian soul than anybody of other nationality - they saw that the American soul is nearer to the Russian than any other one.

They rested here, they became strong once more and with renewed forces go now to the fight for life, which is so hard for the Russian refugees abroad. And during this fight they will always keep in their hearts a warm feeling to the good, kindred soul, which helped them so much in the hard moment of their lives.

Your health, Mr. Smith . . . Hourra . . ."

A Group of Students

"Dear Mister Smith!

We, students of the Practical Technical Academy A. Kh. S. T. L., congratulate you on this holiday of the resurrection of Christ, and on this great day with all our hearts we want to wish you good fortune, health and greater strength for the continuation of your activity for the good of young people and through this activity the betterment of all humanity.

During the entire time we spent in our classes we always felt from you a warm, caring and friendly attitude to us, our interests and needs.

Now we are leaving our studies, and those persons who became close friends, almost like family. Dear Mister Smith, believe that in the depth of our souls we will always retain a warm feeling of gratitude and thankfulness to you, and the time we spent in our courses will be a bright light in our life.

The memory of you and the time spent in our studies will help us during our heavy, lifelong struggle never to lose faith in goodness and in humanity."

CLOSING OF THE SCHOOL
Harvey's statement.

"Near the end of the second six-month course we questioned the Berlin office as to the future of the school. As the YMCA could not support the school any longer, we were asked to consult officials in the Bulgarian government to see if they would absorb the school into their Department of Education. All concurred in the worthiness of the school, but Bulgaria, too, was in dire financial straits. The officials were very complimentary to the school, said that the courses had been very valuable, and they expressed regret that they could not see their way clear to continue the fine work done. We thanked them for their cooperation in helping the International Committee of the YMCA conduct the school for the past two years."

The graduation of 673 students, in the school's two years of existence, attest to its success.

Inquiries were made to private foundations, but funds sufficient to continue the school were not found.

Thus the school had to close.

GOING HOME

"July 18, 1924
Dear Henning,

As you will notice I am sailing and nearly in New York on the *Veendam* . . .

My thoughts reflect back to our good old school. We have wonderful friends in Sofia. The Russians with whom I worked had . . . the greatest sense of justice of any group with which I ever worked. I only met a few Russians in Paris, but they simply do not have the high morality that was ever present in our group.

My hope is that someday these wonderful folks will again be given their chance. If they could be brought together to open a school in Russia proper they would make their most desired contribution to their own country.

The more I reflect over what we were able to accomplish in so short a period in Sofia the more I feel pleased with our efforts. And by the way you need not fear to call on me relative to any little questions should they arise . . .

In these days as I draw away from you all, I have many happy reminders of our work well done and friendships warm. Many good wishes to continued excellent work by all our men in Europe. I regret very much that I will miss Dr. Mott in New York.

Please give my best wishes to all my old friends.
Harve Smith"

ROBERTA IN JAPAN

ROBERTA'S PASSPORT
JAPAN 1926

ROBERTA in JAPAN
1926-1930

Contents

Who is Roberta?...137
History of Japan & Map of Japan 138

Shipboard - August 1926 141
Docking at Yokohama -The Unexpected Happens 142
By Train To Kobe..144
Roberta's Observations - October 1926.............................146

Kobe Y.W.C.A 151
Learning Japanese/Teaching English................................154
Western Cooking Classes..156
Our Japanese House..159

House Cleaning by Government Decree............................161
Christmas 1926 162
Mourning and Funeral for Emperor Taisho 163
Economy and Economic Disparities.................................165

Climbing Mt. Fuji 167

Cherry Blossoms and Azaleas...171
Household Finances..173
Earthquakes...175
Business Girls Clubs...177

Enthronement of Emperor Hirohito 1928..........................179

Girl Reserve Club 189
It's COLD It's HOT 190
Western Sewing Classes...192

Hong Kong - Men Meet Women—1920s Style 193

Day to Day Life 195
Japanese Language Class: Second Year 198
Dinners, Dances and More 199

Nikko - Temples, Kegon Falls, Walking in the Rain 202

Two Friends and Men 207
Fashion—Hats and ? 209
Books and Movies of the 1920s 211

Hokkaido - Farms and an Ainu Home 212

Y.W.C.A. Fund Raising: Traditional and Unique 215
Changing Times for Americans 223

Peking - Summer Palace, Ming Tombs, Great Wall 226

Celebrations 236
Japanese Language Class Graduation Day 238
Flower Arrangement Class and Tea Ceremony 240

Hiking - Fuji San Lakes and Minobu San 243

Teaching Swimming 250
Mushrooms on a Mountain 253
Chrysanthemums and Maple Leaves 254

Thinking About Going Home and Going Home 255

ROBERTA IN JAPAN

Significant differences existed between the experiences of Harvey and Roberta:
- Roberta went to Japan with no prior plans except to participate in the Kobe Y.W.C.A. Harvey had specific Y.M.C.A. programs to implement.
- Roberta was in one country during 4 peaceful years with time for travel and an annual month's vacation.
- Harvey was in 2 countries for only 2 years each, both in political turmoil, with limited options for travel.
One significant similarity - both learned new languages: Roberta - Japanese and Harvey - Russian.

Roberta's Letters

Most of Roberta's letters were to her parents, to whom she wrote several times a month. and many to her college friend, Jae. Usually these letters included references to family and friends and excerpts were taken to describe her Y.W.C.A. work. In letters to others, the recipient is identified.

Roberta's letters usually included only the day of the week and date of the month, e.g. Wed. Nov. 4, without the year, so are not organized chronologically. However, content rather than date is important because her Y.W.C.A. projects were diverse and on-going.

Note: Roberta's letters in this book, and recollections of her experiences, are all in quotation marks.

Background information and explanations which I have written are without quotation marks or within boxes.

Photographs

The photos on dark background with hand printing are from Roberta'a scrapbook she made while in Japan.

WHO IS ROBERTA?

Roberta Anderson was born in 1901 and grew up in a family of seven children in rural Iowa. Her father was one of the Swedish immigrants who had arrived by covered wagon to Iowa.

Having no electricity, their house was heated with a wood stove; kerosene lanterns provided light. Her father delivered mail with a horse and buggy and later started a grocery store in nearby Madrid. She had a happy childhood in a loving family where college was a definite expectation for both daughters and sons.

At the University of Iowa, Roberta lived with her uncle, Carl Seashore, Dean of the Graduate College, her aunt Roberta, and her four cousins. She was on the Y.W.C.A. Council, a member of Alpha Delta Pi sorority and elected to Staff and Circle, the women's honorary society recognizing leadership and scholarship. Her older brother Paul was on the Y.M.C.A. staff and traveling in Europe.

She wanted to travel after graduation in 1924 so applied for and was accepted for a job with the Y.W.C.A. After orientation in New York City, her first position was as a secretary in Grand Rapids, Michigan, while waiting for an overseas job.

She lived with two roommates who were afraid of mice, which appeared sometimes in their apartment. Roberta had grown up in the country so mice were familiar. The roommates said if she set traps for mice, they would do the cooking!

Roberta met Harvey in Grand Rapids, after his return from Bulgaria, and a serious romance evolved. However, before settling down with anyone, she was determined to have her own adventure. Then came the news: she was offered a position as Y.W.C.A. Secretary in Kobe, Japan!

JAPAN

The history of Japan is traced from 13,000 BCE and hunter-gatherer people to 500 BCE when rice cultivation began. The following centuries involved continuing conflicts among shoguns and samurai warriers seeking domination.

In the 1600s the Tokugawa Shogunate gained broad powers and initiated a policy of isolation, except for controlled trade with the Dutch. Japanese were banned from leaving the country and foreigners were banned from entering Japan.

During this period a rich cultural life evolved. Writing had been introduced earlier and sculpture, pottery, wood block prints and Kabuki theatre thrived. Isolation lasted for two centuries until U.S. Commodore Perry appeared in the mid-1800s with his ships and demanded that Japan open trade. Other countries followed.

Emperor Meiji during his reign,1868-1912, abolished the shogun and samurai traditions. His goal of leadership was to modernize Japan in order to stand on equal footing with the Western powers culturally and militarily. His government sent Japanese scholars to Europe to study everything from literature to government to engineering, banking and modern warfare. Western scientists were invited to teach at Japan's new universities. The traditional society was moving in new directions.

Major changes resulted. Japan developed a constitution and parliamentary government and universal education. New railroads were built and new industries developed.

The cultural history of Japan, including theatre, art and religious traditions, continued to be vibrant while the country was engaged in modernization.

The interest of women in Western culture was reflected in activities of the Y.W.C.A. in Kobe.

Reference: *A History of Japan* — R.H.P. Mason & J.G. Caiger

JAPAN in the 1920s

Japan is composed of approximately 3000 islands. The four largest are Hokkaido to the north, Honshu in the center, Shikoku and Kyushu to the south.

SHIPBOARD
August 1926 S.S. *President Taft*

"Dear Mother and Father,

    This is my first letter and of course it's to you. You can probably imagine how I'm enjoying the lazy life on shipboard . . . We passed through the Golden Gate safely and then the ocean became rough. We were all able to go down to dinner however, and through it all we have survived, not one of our party of four getting seasick . . . We sleep until eight or after each morning, then have breakfast. Usually we go for a walk on the promenade deck after it, and then read until lunchtime. Gibbie (a Y.W.C.A. secretary) and I have been sleeping each afternoon and dinner is at seven. It truly is a gloriously lazy life.

    This morning we were very athletic. We played deck tennis for nearly an hour and then they had deck sports which we entered . . . We tried everything and I made final in potato race . . . After the sports had ended we went swimming. The pool on deck is about 20' x 30' or smaller so only two or three can go in at once but we had loads of fun and Oh! how hungry we were at lunch. We've entered the shuffleboard contest and deck tennis tournaments so will have to get in some practice . . . Tomorrow we get to Honolulu where we spend the day. We have radio grammed to the Y sec'y there that we are coming as she has a car and we hope will drive us about. We hope to swim at the beach at Waikiki.

    With loads of love to you,
        Your daughter Roberta"

"Dear Mother and Father,

    Just a note to say we are nearing Japan. At four today we dock at Yokohama. Hazel (a Y.W.C.A. secretary) and I will stay in Tokyo tonight and get on the boat tomorrow for Kobe.

Yesterday we got three radiograms from different folks in Japan welcoming us . . . It reminded us though that our playtime was over and we have jobs waiting for us. You can rest assured that we will be well taken care of . . .

With loads of love, Roberta"

DOCKING AT YOKOHAMA
THE UNEXPECTED HAPPENS

"My darling Mother and Father,

A letter to you on last week's boat was necessarily delayed as I shall proceed to explain now. Promise me first that you will not be alarmed! Have you? All right then.

Imagine your husky, lean, lanky daughter, who wasn't seasick or ill a day on the boat, arriving in her adopted country only to land in the hospital! This is how it happened.

On Monday . . . I wakened with a terrific headache which is unusual for me.

I ate breakfast and lunch but had cold chills all the while I stood on deck gazing at land once more. When the doctor looked us over I managed to keep a stiff upper lip and also have my passport examined, but then I had to go to my cabin. The ship's doctors found I had a fever of 102½ and said I must not get off the boat that night.

. . . The next morning my fever was just as high though the doctor could find no other symptoms than a cold. Miss Scott, General Secretary of Japan, with offices in Tokyo, came back to the boat and it was decided I should dress and go there instead of staying on the boat to Kobe . . . I had my first ride in a "rickshaw". . . from the boat to the interurban.

It took us an hour from Yokohama to Tokyo and we taxied from the station there to the Nitobe House where Miss Scott and Miss Helever live. I don't know when a bed ever felt better!

Rickshaw of the 1920s in Japan

That afternoon a very good Japanese doctor who had studied a year with Mayo Bros. Rochester and a year at Johns Hopkins called and gave me a thorough examination finding it a cold settled in my chest and head. He gave me some medicine which broke the fever about 10 o'clock so I slept like a top only to find my temperature up again in the morning."

> Roberta went back to the hospital for more than a week with chest and ear infections and spent several weeks recuperating at Nitobe House where the first floor was used for Y activities and the upper floor for staff.

". . . I hope you have not been worried since receiving news of my illness. I am well again and that means a great deal. I came back from the hospital Monday to Nitobe House . . . and since then have done nothing at all. Should I complain? In spite of this laziness I am "itching" to get to Kobe.

— • —

I have a great deal to write about my impressions of Japan, the customs, etc. but am waiting until I get at my Underwood in Kobe. I can type so much faster than write long hand . . .

— • —

A 1920s Underwood

I haven't found out how many "Y" people there are in Tokyo and Yokohama but just loads have come to see me. The secretaries throughout Japan whom I haven't met as yet have sent me such lovely notes, hoping for my speedy recovery, and inviting me to their various cities for weekends. Altogether being sick hasn't been as dreadful as it sounds."

BY TRAIN TO KOBE

"Dear Mother and Father,
   At last I am in Kobe, and glad I am to be at last in my own room and in my own clothes again . . . I left Tokyo Thursday morning at 9:30 reaching here at 9:13 that night. I took the day trip because the scenery is lovely and on a clear day, which it wasn't, one can see Fuji, the famous mountain . . . An Episcopal clergyman . . . took the seat in front of me and as he has spent most of his life in Japan I felt secure in knowing that he could help me out if Japanese was necessary.
   We followed the sea from Yokohama for several hours and also climbed many feet into and over the mountains. However there were at least twenty tunnels so we also went through the mountains. The rice fields were profuse and the grain just ready for cutting. We also passed many orange groves and tea fields and of course saw many plots of mulberry trees . . .

Whole mountain sides were under cultivation being terraced for tea plants and even rice fields in small patches quite high up. Very few horses or cows are used comparatively and it would be impossible to get them up the mountain sides so all the work must be done by hand and all the grain carried down the mountain sides by hand . . .

Clare Armstrong with whom I am living was at the station to meet me as well as four Japanese secretaries. They were so gracious in their welcome that it made me feel right at home. At the building yesterday I found a big welcome sign in English to greet me at the door.

My trunks were already at the house so yesterday and today I've been unpacking and straightening up my clothes . . .

This afternoon we are going to a Japanese home to a tea drinking ceremony . . . I am enclosing the program from the movie we went to last night. It was a Japanese movie with horrible scenes and the action so slow . . . There are no words for Japanese movies and a man stands up in front and tells the story as the pictures are shown. The American movie shown after it was good. Of course the Japanese cannot read the words shown on the screen for our shows so this man tells the story of it in Japanese. I think I was more amused at the man than the picture though I could not understand a word he said.

With bushels of love,
Roberta"

HAPPY BIRTHDAY - OCTOBER 23

"Dear Mother and Father,

I have reached the august age of 25. For some reason I do not feel very different from other days . . . Gibbie came down from Tokyo Friday morning . . . We made candy in the evening then walked to the top of the mountain back of us and took pictures by moonlight.

I was awakened Saturday morning when Clare came into my room singing Happy Birthday and at breakfast I found a lovely red Japanese print . . .

Clare had invited about 75 to meet me so there was much preparation. The maid had the house clean but we arranged the flowers and tables, chairs and finishing things. We had gotten some chrysanthemums so planted them in the garden by the walk. I even swept the pond with our goldfish with a queer bamboo thing as in Japan your garden must be swept as well as your house. By 3:30 we were in our best dresses and manners and guests began to arrive. It was a most interesting group and I enjoyed meeting everyone.

You may be interested in hearing what a cosmopolitan group it was. Of course there were many Americans and a good number of Japanese but there were also two Indian ladies with their white scarves draped over their heads, Canadians, English ladies and a lady whose husband is a titled Dutchman. There were about 50 here and the teatime passed very quickly. We served oatmeal cookies, brownies, bread and butter, and cake we had made.

So you see it was a real birthday."

ROBERTA'S OBSERVATIONS

Excerpts from an October 26, 1926 letter Roberta wrote to family and friends on her typewriter with onion skin carbon copies.

"Dear Family and Friends,

 . . . On the boat the constant joke was, what is the title of the book you are planning to write in your first six weeks in Japan? Having been here nearly two months and finding my impression changing and my ideas going through a process of reconstruction at every turn, I cannot see how anyone could have the audacity to attempt a book. It is with fear and trembling that I try to give you an idea of this wonderful country.

Tokyo

... In the cities of Japan one is constantly surprised by the modern things, paved streets, boulevards, large fine street cars, motor busses, beautiful Japanese made and foreign automobiles, traffic policemen on the corners wearing white gloves, and buildings of brick or stone eight and ten stories high. At night all Japan is well lighted for the mountains give the country an immense supply of electricity. However Japan is characteristic in this, that alongside a Packard automobile in which is riding a Japanese family in Western dress, we see men pulling carts piled high with grain or what not, a wagon drawn by a cow with a man walking at the side leading the animal, the wagon having high back wheels and tiny front wheels and the shafts running to a collar or yoke of wood or rope on the animal's neck ...

Bicycles and motorcycles with all sorts of bodies with three wheels are constantly seen. There are sidewalks on the Ginza, the main shopping street of Tokyo, and we have one short stretch of sidewalk in Kobe, but otherwise everyone walks in the road, dodging conveyances, but mostly the conveyances have to get out of the way of the pedestrians. I think the Japanese people go on the supposition that they walked the streets before automobiles came and they are going to keep their rights.

As a consequence each automobile, karuma and bicycle has a bell and automobiles have two horns which are in use constantly ... Many of the streets, in fact most of them, are wide enough for only one automobile so if two meet one has to back out of the street. The drivers here all have to have a license and pass a certain examination so are very skillful in their operation of a car.

One also finds an attempt at blending the ancient with the modern in the dress of the Japanese. Most of the businessmen wear Western dress as many large concerns demand that all employees discard the kimono. The students have adopted a skirt, a large pleated affair that they wear over their kimono and often wear shoes and stockings with the outfit. Girls as well as men wear this and it is sort of a sign of a profession . . . In fact men here wear anything - Western dress, using underwear for outer clothing and sometimes shirts under their kimono.

The women, however, have stuck pretty closely to the kimono. They have lovely materials in them and their obi, the belt worn around the waist, is sometimes gorgeous. On their feet they wear tabi, or a white stocking that just comes to the ankle and is made with a place for the big toe. The geta or wooden shoe has two straps from the front and they hook their big toe into one side and off they trot. Many schools demand uniforms of Western dress and many children wear our clothing so to see a Japanese family together each member may be dressed different.

Kobe

There are a great many Chinese and Koreans in Japan especially in Kobe. There are about 5000 foreigners altogether here which include Russians, Indians, Europeans and Americans. We have a good many Chinese girls in the classes at the Y and I have a number in my classes . . .

Kobe is one of the most foreign cities in Japan as it has a fine harbor and the shipping business brings in people of every nation. In nearly every shop one can get things by speaking English which is not true of any other city in Japan. All the school children learn English in school . . .

The city itself is unique and being about a mile wide and I dare not say how long as it blends into Osaka and other cities. It stretches from the sea up to the mountains and each street is a bit higher than the other as you approach the mountain. There are shrines and parks on the mountain sides in the city and from there one gets a most magnificent view.

Kobe in the 1920s

Kobe Harbor

Kobe being such a foreign city supports a Union Church for English speaking people with a splendid minister. I have met a great many fine people there and through it I know will make many friends. Kobe College for Women has a faculty of 60 which includes nine foreigners and as they live only two blocks from us, we do many things together. The Kobe College household as well as the Y.W. household belong to the Fifteen Club which meets every two weeks for social, literary and musical programs and consists of fifteen English speaking households in Kobe. There are a few missionary families, several Canadian Academy faculty members and a number of businessmen as members. The club has existed for thirty years so the tradition is splendid. There is also a Kobe Women's Club which I hope to join very soon . . .

Kobe has a theatre street where both Japanese and American movies are shown . . . We have also attended Opera here, a Russian company giving splendid interpretations . . . Last night we went to Osaka to see historic Japanese plays given by a school."

Motomachi Street, Kobe

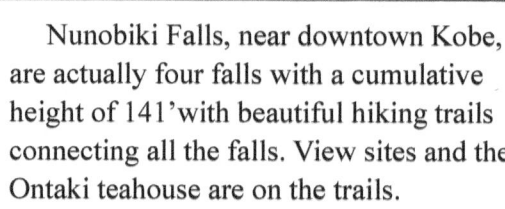

Nunobiki Falls, near downtown Kobe, are actually four falls with a cumulative height of 141' with beautiful hiking trails connecting all the falls. View sites and the Ontaki teahouse are on the trails.

At the highest point is a view of Kobe and the Harbor.

KOBE Y.W.C.A.

"... We have a small association compared with Grand Rapids - five Japanese secretaries and two foreign, an eight room house for our building and the work consisting of English and cooking classes, high school girls clubs, and a bit of business girls work. The work is entirely in the hands of the Japanese secretaries and is at an early stage but is a great step to have it all Japanese. Usually when a secretary first comes out she goes into language school and does nothing in the Association until the second year when she takes on an English class or two. However they are starting me on an entirely different schedule.

Since there are only two of us foreigners here I have had to take on six English classes and a cooking class and next week will add to that five hours of language study a week with a private teacher . . . I have learned phrases and a few words and characters but it will be most interesting to get into actual study. It will be hard I know, but I feel so helpless without knowing Japanese that there will be an added incentive to learn quickly . . .

You who know how I have always avoided teaching must be amused I am doing it in Japan. I have two classes in advanced conversation, one children's class where we play *Farmer in the Dell* and such games, and three beginners classes. It seems strange to get out the old English grammar and review nouns, participles, etc. but I really am finding the teaching interesting.

Roberta and Staff at the Kobe Y.W.C.A.

Standing-Left to Right: Clare Armstrong - Secretary, Terada San - Office Secretary, Roberta - Secretary, Watanabe San - Girl Reserve Secretary, Iwasaki San - Education Secretary. Seated - Left to Right: Siboyashi San - Industrial Secretary, Iniya San - General Secretary

My cooking class meets for the first time this Friday. There are six or eight registered and we will begin by preparing breakfast. All this classwork will have to be done with an interpreter and I am rather anxious for the first meeting to be over but I think I will enjoy it. This noon I am going into the kitchen and make muffins to be sure I remember how they should be.

One strange thing about teaching here is to find all the students rising when I enter the room and bow gracefully. When the class is finished they bow with great ceremony and thank me for coming and teaching them. Imagine a group of Americans doing that!

Perhaps some of you are wondering where the connection is between this English teaching and Industrial work. The situation as far as Industrial work is concerned is very different here and only small beginnings have been made. Kobe has very few industries but Siboyashi San, our Industrial Secretary, does a bit of work in one factory and in a few years hopes to do more of it. Of course the Industrial girls know absolutely no English and until I know Japanese I cannot do anything at all."

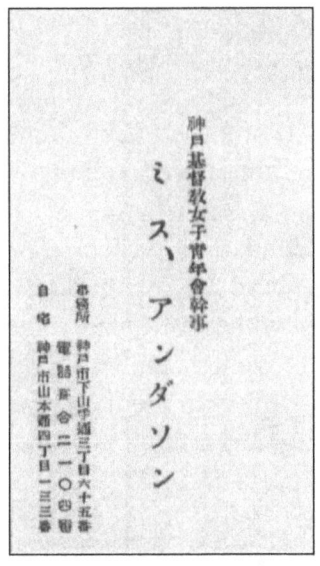

Roberta's cards identify her as a Secretary with the Kobe Y.W.C.A.

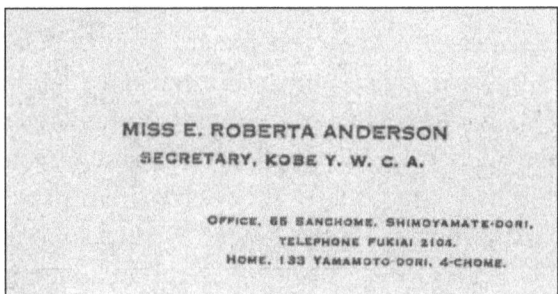

LEARNING JAPANESE
In the Beginnning

"... One day as a downpour of rain came as the children were leaving (from an English class), I had to gather up a number of umbrellas and escort them to the car line. I discovered that little Yoshio lived just up the street a few houses and as he seemed most eager for me to go with him ... I went to his door. After the usual greeting "I have come" his Mother came to the door and insisted on my coming in.

I stepped out of my shoes and Yoshio was very excited as he led me into the living room. It was a hot afternoon and after a cold drink ... was set before me, Yoshio's mother fanned me as she chatted in Japanese. Out of the conversation I gathered only a few phrases, but fortunately I knew the name for dog and flowers so was able to bring in a few sentences which fortunately she could understand. Before I took my leave I went over in my mind the proper words to say and venturing forth with them, I went on into the hall way and getting my shoes again I left."

"Dear Earl, (Roberta's younger brother)
I should be studying for exams beginning next week and I get so sick of cramming in Japanese that I must have diversion. I really do plenty of other things - that's the reason I must work so hard these last few days, for I've played more than I've studied lately. I'm planning to do nothing but study all day tomorrow, Saturday, so I should accomplish something. The Chinese characters about drive me silly though. I can usually recognize them in reading but I certainly can't write them and that's what we are supposed to do. Life certainly takes on a gloomy atmosphere about exam time ... "

TEACHING ENGLISH

"... Teaching English is the first constructive thing that a foreigner can do so many English classes became my responsibility. I taught in both morning and night school and had special classes from a government school and also a children's class . . . My children are so cunning and I do so love that class."
Roberta's report to Y.W.C.A. – Sept. 1926 - March 1927

"Dear Jae, (Roberta's college friend)
. . . You know I don't care much about teaching English. It is all so elementary - I stand, I walk, This is a broom, etc. that I think sometimes I will revolt and say I'll not teach any more at all but then the girls are so darling and invite me to go interesting places with them . . ."

"My dear Mother and Father,
I have just finished teaching three hours of English conversation at the Yamate Girls School . . . for six weeks I'm teaching seven hours a week there for Mrs. Smith while she is in America . . . I have III, IV and V year girls in what would compare to our high school. Some classes have only 25 or 26 but most have 48 and 49. I am teaching conversation so use nursery rhymes, songs with motions and games as well as a book. The principal of the school . . . had the head English teacher write me to not appear in a sleeveless dress so I have my teacher's uniform - a black and white voile with long sleeves - a very sober dress I brighten up with my red felt hat so am able to keep my spirits up . . .
Only it's frightfully cold and I have to wear my winter coat into the classrooms. We haven't any heat at all so I'm thankful I teach only till Christmas . . ."

WESTERN COOKING CLASSES By Request
Roberta's Letters to Her Parents

". . . My demonstration class this term has had its membership change from 13 to 18 then to 21 in the four lessons. This Wednesday I demonstrated apple pie, baking powder biscuits, butterscotch rolls and strawberry shortcake. It certainly kept me busy hustling to make enough in two hours so each one would get a taste. My pie was delicious, the shortcake melted in our mouths so I was happy."

"Foreign cooking classes are very popular in Japan. Besides learning how to prepare foreign dishes the women are most eager to learn table etiquette so in our course we plan to include the latter. It fell to my lot to teach several of these classes and I found them most enjoyable. For my ten lessons of demonstration work, the class was rather formal and I had an interpreter by me as I prepared the meats, vegetables or desserts, whatever the lesson was.

The practical work which followed was the most interesting though. The girls all came in big white aprons which had sleeves large enough to envelop their long kimono ones and prepared a menu which we later sat at the table and ate.

As I am taking Japanese lessons all the time I put some of it into practice in this class and received some splendid instruction there. Many funny things happened as a consequence, for I often used the word cat for beefsteak and similar mistakes, but all the girls were helpful and in two hours we were always seated at a properly set table with one girl serving as hostess and two others as maids.

One day we prepared salad and sandwiches and went up to Nunobiki Falls for a picnic. We went back to one of the girl's homes for tea and enjoyed having her play the samisen (a three stringed Japanese instrument) for us. Such pleasure trips together have made us very good friends."

"... I have 26 in my cooking group ... Last Thursday I made a concoction of Japanese macaroni, tomatoes and bacon like Mother makes at home. They liked it immensely. Foreign cooking is terribly popular here so even to a factory for noon work, I carry my pots and pans and use their hibachi and cook. Yesterday at the Silk Conditioning House we made peanut brittle ..."

"Last week I had a most interesting neighborhood cooking lesson in a beautiful old home with ladies whose husbands are in the Mitsubishi Bank as pupils ... a rambling place with at least twenty five rooms and a roomy Japanese kitchen where the 14 ladies could cook quite conveniently. They all sat on stools or on cushions on the floor while I made an explanation of the menu; then they each made something and we finally all ate our goodies sitting in the dining room, yours truly at the head of the table.

We made Iced Coffee, Boiled Salad Dressing, Vegetable Salad, Chinese Fried Rice, Baking Powder Biscuits, Chicken a la Maryland and they were as pleased as children at learning how to make it all. We prepared it all in two hours so you can imagine we hustled but then all the housewives were used to cooking."

"... If I hurry I can get a letter in the mail so as to make a fast boat tomorrow ... I was at the building at 8 o'clock, had charge of morning prayers for our staff. Immediately after that I took a furoshiki and a shopping list and went to the grocer and market to do the shopping for the cooking class ... We have no ice and very little supply room so everything from flour to ice for ice cream has to be bought and it takes a good hour to do the buying."

Roberta's Letters to College Friend

"Jae dear,

To get my mind off cooking a little while, I'll answer your good letter which came last mail. Honest to Betsy! You'd think I was a Home Ec grad and hoped to teach all Japan foreign cooking by a glance at my week's schedule.

On Tuesday afternoon from 1 to 3, I do demonstration cooking to my class of beginners. Then on Wednesday and Thursday I have the advanced classes which prepare a luncheon and eat it. Today I just finished my noon luncheon when I helped Kawamoto San prepare a Japanese supper for our club girls who come tonight.

Then I had to make a menu for my 22 business girls who chose cooking for their activity on this, their club night. I am making French toast and maple syrup this evening. None of the girls have stoves or ovens, just a little charcoal burner, so I must make very simple things. By the time I go to bed tonight I'll probably be dreaming of the kitchen . . . "

"This week one night I taught a group of club girls how to make candy. We made peanut brittle and had a taffy pull. They thought it heaps of fun and both kinds turned out well."

". . . Last week proved most busy. All the classes began and we have 60 in night school besides a new cooking class of 13 and some other special classes. I have taken on the new demonstration class in cooking and supposedly given up my practical class but the teacher has not been able to be there so last week I taught both of them . . . our Education Secretary was ill last week and also our janitress. With two cooking classes on my hands and both of them gone, I was rather a busy lady. I had to go to the market and buy all the provisions for a dinner for twelve, then talk in Japanese as best I could for my interpreter was gone, and then have all the dishes washed and little odd jobs usually done by our janitress. It all went all right, though."

OUR JAPANESE HOUSE

"Dear Mother and Father,
 I haven't told a thing about our house or my housemate. Clare is a peach and I like her immensely . . .

 The Y.W. house which Clare and I have to ourselves this year is a Japanese house, and is far up on the mountainside, in fact we are the last house on this ridge and we have a wall of cedars going straight up from our back door. The house accommodates four people very comfortably so Clare and I get almost lost in it, however we have a great many guests so it is used extensively. We are constantly meeting boats and taking folks home overnight, etc. etc.
 . . . In my room I have a fireplace but today a wood stove is being put in each room and no doubt will be very welcome . . .
 Next time I write I will describe or draw a picture of the house for you for it is Japanese and very interesting. I have one strenuous objection to it. The doorways are made for Japanese and not for tall Americans and I will either come home a stooped over figure or with dents in my head. As yet, I have escaped the latter but I do not know how long it will last. I honestly touch the top of the doorways when I stand erect in them. I see I should never have come to Japan if I valued my life, especially my head.

View of Kobe harbor from monohoshi of house.

— • —

Another feature of our house is the monohoshi, or platform on top of the house where clothes are hung to dry. Each night before going to bed, Clare and I go out for the lights of the city are beautiful from there and with the gorgeous moon that has been shining on us for the past week we could see as far as in daytime. We have a few clotheslines on our monohoshi but most folks have only bamboo poles on which they put their kimono and underwear to dry. With the sleeves out straight they do not have to iron them.

— • —

My room is a huge one with fireplace, big Korean chest of drawers, two bookcases, large closet and a big desk with five drawers on each side. The room has windows on two sides and the third is all paper doors and looks out over the bay where I can see the ocean liners come in and out, and way across at night the light of Osaka . . . it is only a 15 minute walk from here to the mountain top where . . . there is a lovely park."
With bushels of love, Roberta"

SERVANTS

". . . We have two servants at our house. Seki San, the cook, and her daughter Yoshia San, as maid. We really have six for Cook San has five children and all live with her in the servants' quarters . . . Cook San gives us plenty to eat, a variety of things and watches every penny as though it was her own. Sometimes we ask for certain things and she says we can't have them - if they are too expensive. Each week we give her 10 yen and on Saturdays she gives us an account of every cent. It will be my job soon to keep "Kanjo" the books so I'll learn more about it. Besides getting the meals Cook San sweeps the yard and scrubs the walks every morning. She also does all our laundry work with the exception of sheets, pillowcases, bath towels and large table cloths. We have no machine or tubs so she washes everything in hand in Lux.

Yoshia San begins the day in winter by lighting fires in each of our rooms these cold mornings. She does all the serving and cleaning, mends our stockings, shines our shoes, most anything in fact. Three nights a week she goes to the YW for English class at 6:30. Those nights her younger sister, who is about 12, serves. Yoshia San is in my class . . . I keep teaching her English and she teaches me Japanese so we have fun between us. When I begin to manage the house I'll have to do everything through Yoshia San for Cook San doesn't understand English and my Japanese is still almost negligible."

HOUSE CLEANING by GOVERNMENT DECREE

"In Japan the law requires that you clean house twice a year and the police set the date for it . . . Before Saturday we took down pictures, put clothes away, etc. so that Saturday morning when the two men came to take out the tatami (the mats on the floors) they could raise all the dust they chose - and they did. They wiped down walls and ceilings, pounded the tatami outside, swept (not washed) the floor under the tatami, put it back, washed the windows and put the furniture back.

Then we dusted, hung pictures, put up curtains and made beds and our whole house was cleaned in one day. Our house includes two downstairs rooms, three bedrooms, big halls, maid's room and servants quarters and all of that was cleaned in the one day. Now the police have come and seeing that we are clean put a stamp on our door which tells everyone we are clean."

CHRISTMAS 1926

Emperor Taisho passed away Christmas eve.

"About Thanksgiving time, some of us were working on a pageant to be given by our school girls at Christmas time. After several practices . . . news began coming out almost hourly of the Emperor's serious illness. For a week or so the quiet and stillness of anxiety was felt in everything and finally all plans for Christmas and New Years were given up. Then the Sunday before Christmas the Emperor began to improve . . . All of our Japanese staff live away from home and only two come from Christian homes. After due consideration of the Emperor's illness, they felt it would be all right to go to our house for a Christmas party. I had made popcorn balls, and opened my Christmas package from Mother.

The most fun of the afternoon was dressing me in Japanese clothes and taking pictures of us all. A month ago I had purchased myself a beautiful ceremonial kimono and the girls wanted to know when they could dress me up in real style. I said then that at our Christmas party they might, and then promptly forgot it.

They didn't, however, and even though they had to loan me an obi, and most of the paraphanelia used to fit it, they had loads of fun dressing me. I borrowed our maid's geta for my feet . . . so felt quite decked out."

"About 5 o'clock on Christmas morning we were awakend by a "gogai" pounding on the door who told us that the Emperor had died during the night. This came rather unexpectedly as all reports had been he was improving . . . His Highness was only about fifty years of age . . . His death meant that all gayety must cease, no music could be had and the order went out that every house should put out the flag draped with black."

Roberta in kimono

FUNERAL OF EMPEROR TAISHO
February 1927 in Tokyo

Roberta took a train from Kobe on Friday night to meet friends in Tokyo to watch the funeral procession. With several inches of snow on the ground, it was very cold.

". . . The funeral was Monday and after lunch we donned several pairs of woolen hose, sweaters, coats and galoshes, lighted our tiny furnaces, the little boxes of punk which Japanese wear in their obi to keep warm, and set out for the funeral . . . our taxi could go within a half mile of the section which was reserved for foreigners, so we hiked along the packed streets to our section. The Japanese government was certainly kind to us for they had chairs for everyone in our section, and a temporary house which was heated near there for us to go and get warm. We took puzzles, books, and games to amuse us during our long wait and about five-o'clock ate our sandwiches which we had brought. As six o'clock drew near, everyone put away his lunch box, book, etc. to be prepared to sit in silence . . . About five-thirty the soldiers who had been lined up near us stepped out onto the newly gravelled pavement which had been sanded since traffic had stopped in the afternoon. The sun which had been keeping us warm had set and the darkness gave a solemn touch to the dimly lighted streets.

Promptly at six we heard the boom of the distant salute on the palace grounds. The soldiers, sailors and their bands playing the funeral dirge, written especially for the occasion, started marching to the Shinjuku station, a distance of four and three-fourth miles from the palace where the procession began . . . Since it was a Shinto funeral, all the priests came in strange old costumes which had always been used on such occasions . . . The ancient ox-cart drawn by four coal black oxen held the Imperial coffin . . . It had two seven-foot wheels which have seven sonorous tones . . . Of course the catafalque was heavily guarded . . . followed by Prince Chichibu, representative of the Emperor . . . There seemed to be hundreds of dignitaries in full costume . . . When the last soldier passed our seats, we had seen 8,000 marchers . . . We had to walk home but didn't mind it a bit for our feet were almost numb. . . . Japan is getting away from many of her old ceremonial things and the present Emperor is very modern in our sense of the word. The Diet appropriated an enormous sum for the funeral expenses which the Emperor cut in two. I doubt whether there will ever again be as ceremonial a funeral as this one."

ECONOMIC DISPARITIES
Poverty

"... No doubt you have read in newspapers about Kagawa San, the great social worker of Japan. On Sunday morning at six-thirty he gave the sermon in the slum district of Kobe to his workers and I went down to hear him. He has a great following and is a wonderful speaker, in English as well as Japanese, but I thought his Japanese was beautiful.

After the service one of the men took me through the slums and it's made me almost ill ever since. When I say truly that the people sleep in shifts, you can understand what poverty there is. I also visited a Gov't nursery where the children were kept during the day while the mothers worked. The charge is 8 yen or 4 cents per day per child which includes the noon meal or milk (some were tiny babies in cradles.) This building was very clean and had eight workers to care for the 120 children who are taken there each day. It is certainly most distressing to visit the slums in any country and feel that one can do so little for them. I was mighty glad of the opportunity to go down Sunday."

Wealth

"Dear Mother and Father,

I delayed writing this week until your letter should arrive but I notice that there have been severe storms on the Pacific delaying the boats . . .

Last Friday I saw a most interesting display of a trousseau. A Japanese girl of a great deal of wealth invited us to her trousseau tea. We were ushered into their lovely Japanese home and found room after room filled with beautiful kimono, haori under-kimono, tansu (dressers), bedding, jewels, etc. There were at least 150 kimono with as many haori coats and obi - simply an appalling number. No human being could wear as many things as she had and it seemed wicked to spend the money and let the dresses just mold in the store house. There were three beautiful wrist watches, at least 15 highly carved amber colored hair ornaments, some tortoise shell ones and many rings. I truly have never seen so many things together outside of a store. The wedding kimono outfit alone probably cost several thousand yen. The daughter is to live next door to her mother so a ceremony of taking all the things to her new home was held a few days after the display - with more money to be spent. Of course the whole thing is to display their wealth . . ."

1927 Financial Situation

"Dear Mother and Father,

. . . At present the financial condition in Japan is rather precarious. About a week ago one of the biggest companies in Japan failed and since then, day by day, banks have been closing their doors. Finally on Friday all the banks over Japan closed for three days until help could be given to those banks who were hardest hit. Then a moratorium was declared for three weeks so that by the time that is up, the conditions all around should be better. The government had rather a difficult time over it all for the party in power did not wish the government to give aid to the failing companies and the Emperor wished it. As a protest the prime minister and the whole cabinet resigned and the party of the opposition is in power. I am banking with the National City Bank of New York which has a branch in Kobe so my few pennies I have there each month are safe. I do have a bit of savings in the Mitsubishi Bank, however, but that is as safe as the government. I feel very sorry for the many people who have lost a good bit and for the Japanese in general for the yen naturally dropped a great deal."

CLIMBING MT. FUJI

"Dear Mother and Father,

I've been up to Fuji San - the highest peak in Japan! . . . Doris and Ruth Cunningham are B.I.J. (born in Japan) daughters of missionaries in Tokyo and ages 27 and 20. We with two others left Gotemba at 8 a.m. by bus to Subashiri where we mounted horses at 9 and rode to the 5th station which took us until about 3 o'clock in the afternoon. We had two guides for our party of five who carried our luggage and stayed with us the whole journey. The ride up the mountain was gorgeous for we rode through woods with gorgeous views of the country.

Mt. Fuji is 12,388' - the highest mountain in Japan and an active volcano which last erupted in 1707. It is a sacred symbol of Japan with temples and shrines around and on the summit.

There are rest houses (stations) along the way and we stopped at each one to eat a bite and rest. The walk from the 5th station to the top took us four hours. It was less than 3 miles but "zigzagged" straight up to the top. We didn't reach the summit in time for the sunset but we saw the beautiful colors on the clouds below us as we climbed along.

The day was hot when we left Gotemba but it was freezing cold at the top. We had high shoes, two pair of wool hose, knickers, sweaters, leather jacket and rain coats plus hats with towels tied over them for warmth and then nearly froze up. We slept at the top in a hut and slept in everything but our shoes, adding another pair of socks, and another towel to our head then crawling in between heavy "futons" on the floor. I was the "filling" for the "Cunningham sandwich" and shivered all night so the cold plus the fleas didn't give us much rest.

We were up before four and outdoors immediately for we had no dressing to do and sat in the shelter of a huge lava boulder to watch the sunrise. It was a gorgeous fiery one and we could see for miles and miles in every direction as the sunrays cleared away the mist. Oh! words simply can't tell the glory of it all. After a light breakfast (I was the only one of the five who felt all right, the air was so thin), we took the two hour walk around the crater.

I think I forgot to say that this sacred mountain is an extinct volcano and as we went about there were hot places in the ground and rocks, so hot we couldn't sit for long, but it felt mighty good to have a touch of something warm for a second. Around and in the edge of the crater there are shops, temples and a post office from which I sent you a card. There are small monuments of lava stone, tiny ones standing everywhere on the crater, and it is said that when parents lose a child they climb Fuji and erect this pile of stone in memory and for penance.

At the temple on top I had a stamp put on my leather jacket as well as on my stick which I had stamped at every station as we went along. It was so very cold we didn't care to linger there long so at nine o'clock we began <u>sliding</u> to the bottom. I think I can best describe the slide saying it was . . . <u>four miles straight down</u>, then another four miles with a little less steep angle and fewer cinders. Over our high shoes we put straw sandals (wore out two pair before halfway down) and wrapped leggins to our knees. It was great fun sliding down for we took steps about four feet in length and sort of bounded along. Our guide had a great time keeping up with us and he thought my stride was dreadful but he explained his legs weren't as long as mine.

The "basha"

From the first station to Subashiri again we took "basha" which means "horse wagon." It is a two wheeled cart affair drawn by a horse and can carry eight people. By taking this vehicle we had tried every means used for going up Fuji though we all agreed we would much rather have walked.

At three we were back in Gotemba feeling fit as a fiddle and joyful because of our happy trip. Doris, Ruth and I claimed our baggage and went over to Minooka where there is a clubhouse and put on our swimming suits and had a good swim . . .

Doris and Ruth are as fine travelling companions as I could find and we're having a heap of fun together though we'd not met till last week. It's rather fun going about this summer sort of on my own for in that way I can join anything that comes up and suits my fancy.

      My love to you all
      Roberta"

CHERRY BLOSSOMS and AZALEAS

"Dear Mother,
 . . . Yesterday I went to a friend's house to a garden party and she had some gorgeous tulips, azaleas and camelia in bloom. A Japanese garden is simply beautiful with its rocks, mounds, stone lanterns and steps so that even without the flowers it is lovely and think how fine the color of the spring flowers make it!"

". . . On Monday folks arrived (Y.W.C.A. friends from U.S., China and Syria) and Tuesday the cherry blossoms were at their height so we had the cook make up eight or nine lunches and we all went out to Suma to view the blossoms. There the trees circle Suma Lake and it is a park that nestles close to the mountains. After viewing the blossoms from all angles but the center of the pond, we chartered a highly decorated boat, with a cockatoo head at the bow, and were rowed about in the lake as we ate our lunch. It was a most beautiful sight, the trees all masses of white against the evergreen clad mountain. I'm sure I was as enthusiastic as anyone for it was my first cherry viewing expedition."

Roberta in a friend's garden.

"... On Saturday after a strenuous week and with the last of our guests just departing, I so wanted to stay at home and rest, but I had promised some girls to go to Korakuen to see the azalea with them. It proved to be one of the most beautiful sights I have ever seen so I am thankful I went . . . I think Japan is the only place where one can find a mountain covered with the lavender azaleas nestled among the pine trees. Words simply can't describe the beauty of it all. Most people think the cherries are superb but I think I shall never see anything more gorgeous than the azalea. . . . From the inter-urban station we took a taxi for a long way till the road ended, and then we climbed on and on to the top with the azalea on every side . . . it was there we ate our lunch and rested for the sun was scorching hot and the climb was a good one. I will just say that the picture in my mind of Korakuen can never be erased."

"... The girls with whom I climbed Saturday are rather favorites with me so I thought that going to Futatabi on Sunday with some night school girls would be rather an anti-climax, but it wasn't. Just four of us climbed this mountain back of Kobe and we really had a great time. They are fourth year students so speak English quite well. We had great fun singing a new Japanese song they had just taught me and then we would swing into some English ones. The Japanese girls love to hike and I enjoy it too so go with them whenever they ask me. Even with groups who do not speak English well I enjoy myself, for I can understand simple conversation and get in a few words now and then."

HOUSEHOLD FINANCES

"Dear Mother and Father,

    I think I have written you about our new house. Last Friday when his H. M. the Emperor visited Kobe we sat on our parapet and watched the battleship come into the harbor escorted by several gunboats firing salutes. Then in the evening the ships sent out fireworks and colored lights over the city which was especially lighted up for the occasion . . ."

"My dearest Mother and Father,

    . . . soon I will have been a year in Japan. I am so glad you ask questions for it is hard to know just what to write . . . and there are so many things to tell. You have wondered about all our guests so I'll explain our house system.

The foreign secretaries in each city have a house, the rent being paid by Foreign Division, N.Y. Our house rent is 175 yen. Then whoever lives there keeps up the house taking care of everything else. Oh yes, beds and necessary furniture is provided by N.Y. too. This winter Clare and I have been alone in our house so we've been paying y110 or $60 each month each. That pays our servants y62.50 and everything.

Each house then works out its own rates for guests and transients. For instance, the Osaka sec'ys at Shukagawa and we go back and forth anytime and do not pay. However, Kyoto folks pay .75 per meal and .25 overnight when they come down. They come to Kobe to shop, meet boats, etc. so our return visits wouldn't balance. Any other Y.W. people in Japan pay us y3.50 per day. Y.W. sec'ys from other countries pay y5.00 per day and others y6.00. When Clare or I go to other places we pay their rates.

So you see out of all our guests we have made money. While Nat'l pays our house rent, the guests use our bed linen etc. and are a bother to us, so we deserve the profit. As a consequence this month we each paid only y60.00 and the surplus paid the extra y40.00 for each of us, bought our summer coal and our ice tickets. During August while we are gone we'll simply have to pay the servants. I hope this makes our house finances clear . . ."

> Roberta handled the household accounts.

"Dear Mother and Father,
　　　. . . I straightened up Kanjo, family accounts, and what a job it is. Our cook pays all the bills, but they must be accounted for and as they are all written in Japanese they have to be translated. I certainly get to use my Japanese by talking to the Cook . . . "

EARTHQUAKES

"March 1927
Mother and Father dear,

    Just a note on the boat which leaves tomorrow telling you that I am safe after the earthquake which struck Kobe last night.

    A friend and I were walking to the building about 6:30 when suddenly we both felt sick to our stomach and then we realized the earth was moving. The shock lasted only two or three minutes and practically no damage was done in Kobe and only one life lost . . .

    I can't quite describe the sensation but I don't look forward to any more. We went to the "Y" amd everyone was in the street, the safest place. We dismissed classes and told everyone to go home for a second quake would follow, we knew, but not when.

    Grace (Roberta's roommate) and I sat in our living room downstairs with the doors open and read until eleven when we packed a suitcase with the clothes we had taken off, put our slippers and coat handy and crawled into our beds. She slept fine but I must confess my eyes didn't want to close. I did drop off though later, and when I wakened I was sitting on the edge of my bed putting my slippers on. I thought I had dreamed there was an earthquake and then crawled in again. I guess I slept about an hour all night. I was greatly surprised to find this morning that the second shock had been true, not a dream of mine. Today there have been a number of shakes - just the earth settlng but we anticipate no more at present.

    . . . The person who was killed was a passenger on the "California", a round the world boat. Passengers were returning to the boat and seven were on the ladder getting on when the shock came. Three were thrown on to the pier and four into the water between the boat and the pier. Three were rescued but the fourth drowned."

"April 1927
Dear Mother,
  I am getting quite used to shakes now as we've had loads of little shocks ever since . . . No doubt all this year we will be having the earth settle after its eruption . . ."

" . . .Yokohama you know was completely wiped out by the earthquake in 1923 and there are still blocks and blocks of debris but it is being built up rather fast.
  The government subsidizes buildings of schools, hotels, etc. that will put up earthquake proof structures and has made a plan for all the reconstruction that is going on. Of course many companies are still in barracks and it seemed strange to see the sign "National City Bank of New York" over a small wooden structure . . . The YW there is also still in barracks though they have purchased a piece of land and are now raising money for a permanent building . . ."

BUSINESS GIRLS CLUBS

"Today there was a business girls conference at the YW so we made "Osushi" for the girls for their lunch. As there were 50 for lunch we boiled what seemed barrels of rice and had huge platters of the other ingredients. The boiled rice was put in a huge wooden tub and fanned till rather cool with vinegar being added all the time. Then we put in cooked mushrooms, white lily root, "Evening Glory" stems, green string beans. After this had been thoroughly mixed and fanned, huge servings were put on each plate and garnished with shredded omelet, green peas, red fish grated, and black powdered seaweed, and red pickled ginger. Imagine eating that? Well I did, some. It was fun to make it though."

Oct. 19, 1926 - Roberta's first acquaintance with Japanese food

". . . On Sunday, Kobe business girls entertained the business girls clubs from Kyoto and Osaka having an all day meeting. We had to serve two meals to the thirty girls but it being Japanese food it was very easy to do. Kawamoto San, the business girls secretary here, had her family make "Osushi" so all we had to do was to serve it out for noon on dishes, place chopsticks beside it and then cut up the fruit for our dinner. In the evening we had a lunch sent in as you can so easily do here in Japan and at each girl's place we had this box of rice, trimmings and soup and more fruit, so it was very simple.

I had nothing to do with the meeting - the girls took care of everything very nicely, but I was glad it was over. These three cities are so close together that three times each year we meet together and talk over our common problems. The girls love it, both to entertain and to go away for we have plenty of games too, but they did a great deal of thinking for this conference too . . ."

"Yesterday it rained all day and hasn't stopped yet. As it was the first Sunday of the month, the day Kawamoto San and I take our business girls to church, we thought no one would come because of the weather. However, four girls braved the storm, one girl for the first time, going to a church. She didn't know any hymns and while we were waiting at the Y for other girls to come she asked me to teach her some. She was . . . so eager to learn that I gave her my hymn book so she could learn some more songs at home. You know the Japanese have never sung together and to many of the girls the Psalm book represents the only form of music for them. They always carry their hymn books when they go on a hike and want to stop and sing hymns. Next month we will go together to a church in another part of the city so the girls in that vicinity can become acquainted with a church near their home . . ."

ENTHRONEMENT OF EMPEROR HIROHITO
November 6, 1928 Kyoto

"GoTai Ten"– Enthronement – the word that has been on everyone's lips this past month! What significance it has had for the Japanese nation! And even we foreigners who were fortunate enough to have been in this land at this time have had the thrill of seeing some of the festivities and watching a nation rejoice as His Majesty Emperor Hirohito, direct descendent of the sun goddess, Amaterasu, ascended the throne and announced to the world and his ancestors that he is now to rule these peoples. It was not a coronation for a crown was not used, so we had to learn to say enthronement months ago when everyone began talking about the event.

The home of the Imperial Family is now in the city of Tokyo, the East Capitol of the Empire, but according to the Constitution of the Empire, the Emperor must be enthroned in the old Western Capitol, in the city of Kyoto.

Emperor Hirohito 1928-1989

Hence great preparations had to be made for bringing the Royal personages to the Kwansai and for welcoming His Majesty in the old city . . .

About two weeks before the Emperor was due to arrive in Kyoto, Grace and I decided that we would shift our classes for the day and go up (Kyoto is just two hours from Kobe) and take a chance on getting a place to see a bit of the procession at least. Upon writing Mary, the foreign secretary in Kyoto, she informed us that we might have a bed there the night before and said we should come early as the trains would probably be crowded. As Kyoto was crowded with police and inquired of the Y.W. every day just whom they were expecting, we were not surprised one day to have the police from Kobe call at the Association and ask Grace and me all our family history, why we came to Japan, what school we graduated from, our age and a dozen other questions. They had had instructions from Kyoto police to look up our record and as we heard nothing further from them we decided we were fit persons to visit the Imperial City . . .

The Imperial train left Tokyo for Nagoya on Monday, the 5th of November. There is an old castle in that city and the Imperial party spent the night there. The next morning they departed and reached Kyoto at 2 o'clock in the afternoon. It is about 400 miles from Tokyo to Kyoto and the whole line was guarded with soldiers who stood just 10 feet apart, if I remember correctly, making a defense even in the country places.

As we were going up to Kyoto on Monday evening Grace and I decided to take a III class Express train which started from Kobe, for we felt that all of the trains would be very crowded. We had our steamer rugs and then had taken our night things just in a "furoshiki" for we thought a suitcase would be just a bulky thing in a crowd . . . Upon reaching Kyoto Station we began to feel in the spirit of the occasion for we saw the Imperial Entrance at the station open for inspection and crowds had gathered to see the beautiful room with tile floor, marble pillars and it all decorated with gorgeous chrysanthemums.

Much to our delight we found a taxi so we did not have to walk the three miles or so to Mary's . . . and instead we rode in state down the street where the Imperial Procession would proceed the next day. The street is lined with shops but there was no sign of merchandise that evening - everything had been put away someplace, I don't see where, and each house, shop, garden and temple ground opening onto Karasumaru was made a platform for people to sit and watch the procession. The stores had had an extra sloping floor made covered with blankets for their patrons and friends to use. The sidewalk was kept clear but for eight or ten feet at the edge of the pavement straw matting was placed on the cement and people were already taking their places as we rode along at 7:30 P.M. when the Procession wasn't until 2:30 the next day.

The bunting with red and white designs of phoenix and other Enthronement insignia was lovely in the

Watching the Procession

lantern light. At each house throughout Kyoto there hung a lantern, in fact they hung at regular intervals down each street, and these white lanterns with the two red suns and the two characters "ho shuku", meaning "we celebrate", with a red or blue huge umbrella or a branch of pine over each one, made each tiny alley even a gala place . . .

Kaburagi San, the general secretary at the Y in Kyoto, had secured places for Grace, Yamamoto San, and me in a store which belonged to a friend of her landlord. We were grateful for even that much of a connection as we rode down the street the next morning at five o'clock ready to take our places to wait for the Procession. We had to leave our taxi about a block away and then walk down the center of the street which was filled with street cars and taxis trying to get away before six o'clock when all traffic on the street was to stop. At last we came to our shop. There were mobs sitting in front of it so we had to take off our shoes, carry them with us as we walked through or rather over the people sitting in the allotted space on the pavement, then put our shoes on to cross the sidewalk, and remove them again as we reached the store.

There we were greeted by the master of the shop and welcomed, given tags to tie on our shoes and were escorted into the already crowded room to the space waiting for us. As we were foreigners and not used to sitting on the floor we were given chairs which we placed to the back and side of the platform so we would not interfere with the people who wished to go back and forth through the room. It was a warm misty morning and we took off our coats and hats to make ourselves comfortable for the long wait. Our lunch we had with us, also writing paper and books to read, but even that early in the morning and long before the Procession we saw so many things to watch that our books were forgotten.

Among the hundreds of people whom we could see in front of us there were no foreigners so we were not at all surprised to have the police come in and ask us our names and ages (in Japan your age always follows your name in giving any information) and also our address in America, even to house number and street. Most of the foreigners who were there had written to their Embassies and received permits to sit in the Palace Grounds but Grace and I felt lucky to be where we were, with the common people, for there we could see the reaction of the ordinary citizen of Japan to the ceremony.

One of the first things that attracted our attention while waiting was the police taking away four or five young boys who didn't look very happy at being sent out. Then every person sitting outside of the shops was searched, both inside the clothing and in the "furoshiki" or packages they were carrying. Of course there were babies lost and the policemen put them on their shoulders and walked up the street calling the names of the parents. Then there were newspapermen, and officials of the Procession who were dressed in frock coats, silk hats and gloves but who rode bicycles up and down the street to give instructions.

About ten o'clock the soldiers of the National Reserves, not the regular army, came marching up from the station and took their places in two rows across the street from us . . . A funny thing - an officer came along to inspect the soldiers in place across the street from us and we noticed that he stopped in front of an elderly man who was wearing a great many medals. After he had gone on, this man hurriedly looked down at his uniform, buttoned and unbuttoned his pockets, etc. and wondered what could have been wrong. I think the officer was just interested in his many medals.

Each man in the back row of the soldiers carried a flag and they practiced a great deal in dipping them and raising them just as the Emperor would go by thus making a wave of flags. Then of course we could not expect the Imperial Party to ride down the street on the plain pavement. Every five or six feet there was a bag of clean sand the length of the avenue and about twelve o'clock some coolies came to spread it out and to brush it smooth with brooms.

While all these preparations were going on we noticed that the nice policeman out in front of our section kept looking at us a great deal. Finally he came in and informed us that we might sit on the chairs even when His Majesty went by because we were used to sitting on chairs and it would not be disloyal to do so. We had planned to "suwarimasu" (sit Japanese fashion) during the procession but after having word from the "mighty" police (they are Authority) we began to put aside our books, writing paper, lunch papers and thermos bottle, and to sit square on our chairs. Later on we saw a policeman talking with our nice one and they both gazed intently at us so we felt that they were discussing whether it was really all right, but as they didn't come in again we felt assured as to our position.

An hour before the Procession was to come (Their Majesties arrived at the Kyoto station at two o'clock) people began to talk in whispers and the police came around to give us instructions as to what to do and what not to do. There was to be silence, no shouting of the "Banzai" meaning literally 10,000 years, but also Hurrah, no smoking or drinking, no thrusting out of the head and shoulders to see better (this he illustrated) and many other do's and don'ts. Then he proceeded to have one woman comb her hair, a man to take off his hat, another man to straighten his "haori" and put his "furoshiki" out of sight. The people in the very front were to hide their shoes and sit squarely. Watching all this go on, Grace and I too sat up straight, square to the front, and talked in whispers lest we should be considered disloyal.

The beautiful horses, carriages, and men to carry the Kashikodokoro had gone from the Palace to the station so we were able to see them before the actual procession. May I say here a little about the Kashikodokoro. In every Japanese household, especially in all families who believe in the Shinto, the national religion, there is a God shelf, a tiny or large shelf placed either in the "tokonomo" or in any room in the house, on which is placed the family shrine. Here candles are burned before the tablets of the ancestors who have died and here prayers are made to the spirit of the ancestors.

Shintoism, being the national religion, in the Imperial household there is a shrine also and must go with the Emperor always. It is called "Kashikodokoro." The box in which it was enclosed was perhaps three feet square and it was carried on the shoulders of the specially chosen men from the village of Yase, just outside of Kyoto, who are always the ones to do such services for the Royal Family.

At two o'clock, as we were all sitting quietly and talking only in whispers, we heard the twenty-one salutes which told us that His Majesty had arrived at the station. Then we all waited breathlessly for the approach of the first of the Imperial Guards on horseback. At twenty minutes of three they came, the guards, the assistant masters of ceremony, then the Grand Master of the Ceremonies, each in separate carriages, the Emperor's Special guard, the Kashikodokoro carried by men dressed in blue and white costumes with special straw shoes and black Shinto hats, then the Emperor's flag and after more special guards, the Emperor himself in a lacquer carriage bearing the Imperial crest and with the phoenix at the top.

His Majesty saluted to the people as he rode along. The Empress followed the Emperor in her special carriage and then came Princes and Princesses of the Blood, a few high officials, Premier Tanaka, and the commanders of the Army and Navy. It all lasted only ten minutes, that is, it took only that long for the procession to pass a given point but it took forty-three minutes to reach the Palace.

I can't begin to describe the carriages and costumes of the personages in the procession. I can only say that the golden saddles and purple nets on the horses, the red velvet trousers, "colonial" shoes and plumed hats of the outriders and footmen, and the gold epulets, bands and trappings of the officials seem like a bit of Fairyland. In our tales of Knights and Princes we read about such things but to have it actually happen in real life and to be privileged to see it was a rare treat.

We were interested in watching the crowds around us as the Procession came. There was utter silence from the time of the salutes till the Procession had passed and the thrilling thing was when the Kashikodokoro passed by. As this is brought out only once in the life time of an Emperor, believers in Shintoism consider it one of the deepest religious experiences to even view it covered as it passes by. As it appeared every person in front of us bowed low and respectfully and we found ourselves doing it too. I am sure many prayers were uttered in the hearts of the people and many old men and women felt repaid for their night of waiting by having this privilege. When His Majesty the Emperor appeared there was another low bow by everyone, for to some he still is a God, or at least a representative of the Gods on earth.

When the Procession was blocks up the street, it may have even been within the Palace grounds, we were permitted to leave. With many low bows of thanks to the Master of the store we departed with the crowd to wander homeward, walking several miles to our house for every taxi had been commandeered . . ."

THE EMPEROR ASCENDS THE THRONE
Imperial Palace November 10 Kyoto

"On the afternoon of November 10th, the Emperor ascended the throne and announced to the world and to the Imperial Ancestors this fact. At exactly three o'clock, when this was finished, Premier Tanaka shouted "Banzai" three times and it was then taken up by the foreign envoys and members of the Imperial family inside the Palace, then by the waiting multitude outside the Palace gates and the 70,000,000 loyal subjects took up the echo and shouted their "Banzai" wherever they happened to be. Taxi drivers were to lead their passengers in shouting as were the little bus and streetcar conductors and someone in every group.

Imperial Palace Gate, Kyoto

We were in Kyoto on that day too and stood just outside the Palace gate so we heard the original "Banzai" of the people inside the Palace and then joined our voices with the waiting crowds. A newspaper man snapped a picture of us so we found ourselves in the "Mainichi" a few days later.

We were fortunate in having been near the gate for immediately after the ceremony all the foreign envoys with their wives came out of the gate riding in their beautiful cars and wearing their court costumes, all the members of the Imperial family staying outside of the Palace, came wearing their several layers of kimono and the women with their hair done up in a queer fashion with a jewel or something on the forehead. Prince and Princess Chichibu passed only ten feet in front of us. A newspaper man beside us pointed out the other persons to us so it proved to be a very thrilling afternoon.

That evening all Kyoto joined in a lantern procession and marched through the Palace grounds. There were 8000 people, the newspaper said, carrying red lanterns and singing an Enthronement song . . . We went to the roof of the Kyoto Hotel and from there we could see the millions of lights throughout the city, the special lights at the big Exhibition and the huge searchlights sending their rays to light up the sky.

But Kyoto wasn't the only city to be illuminated. I have never seen such beautiful lights as were sent out from the warships anchored in the Kobe harbor. Several nights it was cloudy and the colored rays upon the clouds were the loveliest thing ever. One night we had a "monohoshi" party, after dinner all of us sat on the "clothes drying porch upstairs" and watched the lights play in the sky and on the mountains beyond. In the streets of Kobe there were hundreds of small parades . . .

Think of me during the holidays as enjoying a trip through the Palace grounds and halls in Kyoto, for it will then be opened to the public.   —Roberta"

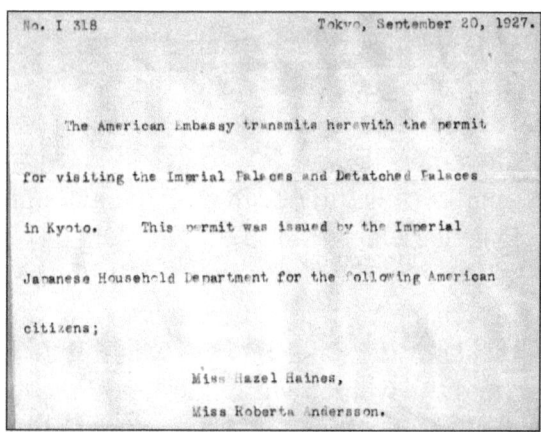

The American Embassy transmitted this official permit from the Japanese Imperial Household Department for Miss Roberta Anderson and Miss Hazel Haines to visit the Imperial Palace in Kyoto. Roberta and Hazel used this for an individual visit in 1927 prior to the Enthronement.

GIRL RESERVE CLUB

"Dear Earl, (Roberta's younger brother)
 . . . I'm having a delightful change from studying by organizing a Girl Reserve Club at Canadian Academy this spring. All children of missionaries and foreign business people in Southern Japan come here for school and live in dormitories. 32 of the 45 girls in the High School are members of the club and we are having a great time getting started.
 I just love it for I can go ahead as I used to at home without any language barrier and as their life here is not normal as at home they doubly appreciate it. I'm terribly keen about the girls too so it's great fun."

"Dearest Mother and Father,
 I had my second meeting of the Girl Reserves at Canadian Academy this week and we had 29 there. Out of only 45 in the high school I think that is a fine percent. We had our first business meeting and tried to adopt a constitution . . . The girls are all just darling, of high school age . . . so it will keep me humping to keep ahead of them. They have never had an organization of themselves before so they are just bursting with things they want to do. Since I had never done Girl Reserve work at home and their program is so different from the Industrial Clubs, I've had to do lots of studying and reading.
 I just love it though, for it is just as though I had stepped across the Pacific to be with a group of English speaking girls. We have another business meeting this week and then they want a cooking lesson. All these girls have been brought up here with servants so they know very little about housekeeping the way we do it at home and are keen to get into the kitchen. Some good things are in store for us all."

IT'S COLD

"... It has been so cold these days that our water pipes burst, but we have no more heat than our tiny stoves in our rooms . . . by using about four buckets of coal a day in <u>each room</u> one could be a bit warm, but with coal at 14.25 a ton we dislike using so much. At the building though is where we freeze. Four of my classes are held in unheated rooms. But then - I'm here - and I like Japan and I mustn't complain but I think now you understand what things we must get used to."

"Saturday last was the end of the "Big Cold," and to celebrate Setsubun the 10,000 stone lanterns and bronze temple lanterns at Kasuga Shrine in Nara are lighted . . . The night was cool and crisp but the moon shone gorgeously through the tall stately cryptomeria trees and we joined the throng filing up the steps to the temple, offering prayers, then returning, rejoicing much as they.
 Beans were for sale everywhere for on that day too everyone scatters them throughout the house to drive out the evil spirits.
  Love, Your daughter Roberta"

"My dear Earl, (Roberta's younger brother)
 It's snowing outside and terribly cold so a good day to stay in . . . My desk is moved close to the little soft coal stove I have in my room in winters and I can conveniently use the toe of my shoe to open or close the draft and it's only a step to the coal bucket. You will be surprised at my skill in tending fires when I return, for while the maid builds the first fire for me to dress by, I tend it carefully through the day. In Kobe snow very seldom covers the ground . . . but it gets mighty cold. There is such a piercing dampness that I find it necessary to wear wool things all winter. The summery warm Japan is all a myth . . . I'll write again . . . this carries New Years wishes from one who loves you.
  Your faraway sister, Berta"

IT'S HOT

". . . Today the sun is blistering hot after a cool spring in general. The sun is so hot that we have to wear hats and carry umbrellas every day. I scorned the warning at first for it is such a nuisance to carry an umbrella but the heat gives one such a headache that I've begun to do as everyone does."

Newspaper Photo: 3rd Year of Showa Era 1929, Vol.16, 180, page 11 "Cool Summer Figure" Kobe NakaYamdte Street

"Mother and Father Dear,
　　How do you like your daughter in the limelight? Kawamoto San found the enclosed picture in the newspaper yesterday under the title "a cool summer figure." I was going out to the Canadian Academy and while about to get on the train I noticed a man take a picture but hadn't an idea it was I who he was taking, but here I am. It was a hot day and I was dressed in white with my pink Chinese umbrella. Thought you'd like to see me."

WESTERN SEWING CLASSES By Request

"Dear Mother,
   ...This has been a frightfully busy day. I taught English two hours at morning school and then went to the Silk Conditioning House where I taught sewing during the noon hour to about forty girls... I know you must think the world is coming to an end when you read that I am teaching sewing! Last week the girls there asked if I would show them how to make some simple summer dresses as their kimonos are so hot and in a rash moment I promised.

   Today I took down some of my simple dresses from which they cut patterns, then I cut out a slip for one girl who had brought material. Next week I must take down a whole outfit of clothing so they can see what to wear under foreign dresses. I was simply petrified teaching this noon (Kawamoto San wasn't there so I had to do it all in Japanese) but it never occurred to me to say that I couldn't teach it. One certainly never knows what will come next in this land! I only wish you were here Mother dear to give me a few lessons both in sewing and cooking."

   "... I'm having a great time teaching sewing to my girls at the Silk Conditioning House and today when I cut out about the 17th dress I felt quite expert. I don't dare wear any complicated dresses down there for they want to copy all my clothes. (I'm probably the only foreigner most of them know.) The green voile with the ruffle has been tripled and tripled again and the white silk broadcloth I brought out with me has been copied as many times. Those two being the only kinds I know how to make I have taken only them down. Next week I think I'll plan some interesting games and try to get their minds off my clothes for it's getting beyond me I fear."

HONG KONG
Men Meet Women —1920s Style

"Jae my dear,

I believe I wrote you about our officer friends from the "Choko Maru" and their pursuit. For a week we played around with them, the outstanding events being a moonlight trip to the "Peak" which truly was marvelous and a ride around the island just as the sun was setting and the moon rising - another evening. The boys were just youngsters . . . It was fun playing around with them but at present prospects for better fun are looming up.

I think I wrote that we are staying at the Miller House, a home for missionaries and are occupying a front room with balcony. The flat across the way has many interesting people and we have noticed in particular two gentlemen, directly across, who seemed to take in everything we did. The other afternoon we were dressed in our new voile Filipino dresses reading on our balcony when the boy brought a note addressed to "The Three Ladies." In it comment was made as to where we might have gotten our "charming frocks" and was signed "of the flat opposite." Our reply was very vague but also in poetry and we were of course greatly amused.

Yesterday morning a huge envelope was delivered to us by the same boy and he waited for an answer. This note was a long poem, cleverly written, in which they asked us to meet them at Lane Crawford's for tea. It was most original and above the tone of flirtation so we knew they were gentlemen and replied that we'd meet them there at four. Gibbie drew pictures of us with names under by way of introduction. Soon a note came back from them giving their full names - added to Doctor and Parson signatures of the previous epistle. At four we met and together sipped tea.

We discovered that they were really the doctor and parson of "King's own Scottish Borderers" about 1600 British soldiers stationed here. They were perfect gentlemen in every way and said they had seen us and could find no other way by which we could meet. After tea they took us to a soccer game between Co. F & G which the Parson refereed.

This morning a note came inviting us to go swimming at Repulse Bay "meeting at or between our respective doors at 2:20." Now isn't this a plot for a story, Jae? The best part of all is that they know we are living in a missionaries home, that we came from Japan, but they don't know what we do. They really think we are idle rich drifting about and as yet we just haven't let Y.W.C.A. slip into our conversation.

You would like the Parson especially as we all do - tall, brown hair and lovely eyes, a bit athletic looking with a fine manly face. In his "shorts" refereeing the game, he quite carried us all off . . ."

" . . . The romance with the gentlemen . . . proved most interesting to the last when they waved us goodbye at the pier. We went swimming, shopping or tea or walks or all every day and our sailing time came too quickly."

Hong Kong photo by Roberta

DAY TO DAY LIFE

"My dear Mother and Father,
   . . . Tonight I am sitting with my machine (typewriter) in my lap out in the roka, enjoying the most gorgeous moon over the harbor. Honestly, from my room I get the most wonderful sunrises and moonlight that I have ever enjoyed. It is hot and sticky tonight but still a small breeze creeps up to us from the sea so that we are not uncomfortable. We certainly do have a choice spot to live . . .
   I love you heaps and am happy to know that this moon I am watching tonight also shines over you.
          Your daughter"

". . . Speaking of Christmas presents. I've nearly walked my legs off trying to find some bedroom slippers without heels to wear at the office. We have to remove our shoes and the building is cold. I have a pair of sandals which are like nothing. If you can find some warm slippers with leather outside and no heels they will be most welome. I wear a 5 1/2 or 6 shoe. I hope you are both feeling well and happy. I am.
          Your loving daughter, Roberta"

"Our president entertained the staff for lunch on Monday at her home and we had a Doll Festival dinner consisting of red rice, "tsukushi" a fresh green picked in the mountains, bamboo, mushroom, fried shrimp and special soups. It was all delicious but the raw fish which I yet cannot eat as a delicacy. After dinner we walked into the hills and found the azalea in bloom. When we returned we had tea in the garden then came on home . . ."

"This week is flying by so quickly. I go out for dinner tonight and tomorrow night, Mac (an American friend working in business in Japan) and I go to a friend's for the evening, Friday a tea, then Saturday I entertain my cooking class girls here. Sunday I'm going to Akashi to a Japanese friend's home to see the cherry blossoms. It is two hours from Kobe and think I'll invite Mac and we'll drive.
With dearest love, Roberta"

Before leaving for Hong Kong:
"It is so hot that we ring water from our underclothing and the dampness that we have always in Japan makes shoes, books and most everything grow "whiskers." This morning I put all my shoes out to air and had to brush off green mold from them all. Books too get a coat of mold so I must wrap all of them in paper and put them away before I leave. I have a bag for my winter coat and have taken very good care of it But that's enough for the weather."

". . .We're so glad to have a heavy rain today for we are on water rations, being able to use it only two hours each morning and evening. They cleaned one tank, or rather emptied the water to mend it, and counted on the rain to fill it and the rain didn't come."

"My darling father,
Your belated birthday gift is at last purchased and I'm putting it in the mail tomorrow. We cannot buy "Ami" in Kobe and I did not get to Osaka until yesterday but now you will surely receive it. When it comes, cut each piece in two crosswise and sandwich in some English walnut meats, then roll again in powdered sugar and EAT. It is a real Japanese candy and I do hope you will like it. My love goes with it to wish you many more happy birthdays!!!!!"

". . . Tonight the *Taft* gets back to Kobe on its way to the States and I am to have dinner with my friend, the Engineer."

"... Today I just finished up my income tax report and tomorrow will have to go to the Consulate to get it signed and then in the mail by March 15. As my salary comes from the U.S. I have to fill it out ... This year I must pay $4.28 and I've collected all the American money in the house to do it. I could get it at the bank but the exchange is wrong for that."

"Dear Mother and Father,
 ... You asked about eating fresh fruits here. The Japanese ... fertilize the gardens with human waste and it breeds more germs than other fertilizers. As a consequence we all get worms here. Next week I take my yearly physical examination and I expect to find myself having them so will take a couple of days off and use the "dynamite" as we call the medicine and get rid of them. This is a dreadful thing to write but everyone here has them and why be silly about it."

"I've also become a typewriting teacher. Last year I gave our maid lessons and now she has a position as typist downtown. Now Shikami San, one of our secretaries, wants to learn so I'll give her lessons at the Y and she can practice on my machine there ..."

"Dear Mother and Father,
 ... Yes I am taking care of the amount I/O Carl (Roberta's older brother) immediately. I am getting along slowly and will be a free woman when I return if all goes well."

"One of our staff, Terada San, is going to the States next month having received a four year scholarship at Huron College. As she has never worn foreign clothes, I am busy taking her to the tailor and the shoemaker and giving her as much time as I can to prepare her for living abroad. When I get home I hope she can come to Madrid to spend a vacation."

JAPANESE LANGUAGE CLASS
Second Year

"Dear Mother and Father,
 This year in school our teachers thought it would be good practice for each of us second year students to lead chapel at school in Japanese so made out a schedule for us. Today was my turn to do it so this is a red letter day for me - my first Japanese speech. I worked hours and hours on it, wrote it all out in Japanese, and then had it corrected by one teacher, practiced saying it over and over and before the 13 people of the school I read my sermon. I think I have never been so scared in my life but I shouldn't have been for I simply had to read it.
 It was three typewritten pages long and thought I would pass out before I had it finished but I survived and my teacher complimented me on it afterwards so I guess I'll attempt my second turn without so much fear. Before the year is out I must appear once more and then I hope never have to speak again . . . I didn't attempt a prayer for one must use literary language in it and I have made up my mind that I will never do it in Japanese so am not bothering about that. Besides the talk, we sang a hymn and said the Lord's prayer in Japanese and that was all. Isn't it fierce to be studying such a difficult language?"

". . . Last Saturday evening all language school, 13 of us, entertained our two Japanese teachers at a turkey dinner at our house. We each brought things so that our cook did not have it all to prepare and one girl brought her maid to help our new maid serve.

We had a delicious dinner - fruit cup, turkey (two), sweet potatoes, peas, homemade rolls, cranberry jelly, olives, then a gelatin salad of grated raw carrots and pineapple served with cheese straws, then banana ice cream, chocolate cake, cookies, coffee and candy. In our dining room we can have two tables, one seating eleven and another four. We used red candles, red sweet peas with fresia, then had red hearts (valentines) on the tables for decoration. All looked very lovely.

For entertainment we had music planned and games and we all had lots of fun. Being in school together every day we know each other well so it was sort of a family party . . . I was glad to have them all at our house."

DINNERS, DANCES and MORE
Excerpts from Roberta's letters to Jae

"My dear Jae,

About the most exciting thing I've done since last writing you is to have gone to the Officers Ball on the battleship *Blackhawk,* one of the US Navy ships in port for a week . . . It was a gorgeous night, full moon and warm, and while waiting at the pier for the good looking speed boat to take us out to the battleship anchored in the bay, the sea and the city with the mountains behind were simply exquisite in the moonlight. The cruiser was well lighted and the deck was decorated with flags and canvas to cover up all the guns, paraphernalia etc. The officers, simply marvelous looking American men, were there to welcome us and dance - and with music by the ship's Filipino orchestra it was perfect.

There was one difficulty and that was that every foreigner in Kobe - French, German, English - felt herself invited and the ship was packed so it wasn't any fun dancing. I met some fine officers and it was terribly thrilling to be there. The men in their uniforms, gold stripes, cords, etc., the women in evening clothes made a gay picture, but the best part of all was that no wine was served and I saw no one drunk. I get so sick of going to parties (tho' I don't go to many) where all the men hang over the bottles and siphons. I'm glad America has prohibition – not that I'm prudish and refuse cocktails always – but I can't say that I've enjoyed them especially. The party closed at eleven and they sent us all back in the ship's boats – another beautiful ride over the water in the moonlight."

". . . I had a scrumptious time at a buffet supper party the other night . . . a gorgeous home, both foreign and Japanese rooms and an exquisite garden. The daughter who has just been married was in one of my classes and though I'd been invited to her home before I never was able to go. The son has been abroad and speaks English very well. He was married recently to a girl whom I know. The party was really given by the son and his wife and only foreigners were invited.

We arrived about six and after looking at the garden, we were taken into a room where a Japanese artist sat with some fans and we were told to ask him to paint any scene or design on one for ourselves. He was a fine artist and I have a beautiful picture of the curved bridge and stone lantern in the garden on mine.

After a delicious supper of salad, sandwiches and ice cream we were shown moving pictures of both son's and daughter's wedding trousseau and reception. The beautiful clothes were undescribable really and Oh! how I wish I might take home some pictures . . . The older folks went home about ten but the rest of us stayed for bridge and dancing . . . "

"... Yes we play bridge out here a lot. Most folks play for money but usually there are some tables where they do not and I play there ... One time we taught a Japanese man how to play and it was heaps of fun playing all in Japanese - calling spades, hearts, etc. in Japanese."

"I was interested in your evening with "cork tips." Do you smoke a great deal? Of course out here nearly everyone does but the missionaries, and while we were on our trip this summer and on the way out I indulged rather heavily ... I rather enjoy it occasionally but am not as fond of it as some are. It is difficult here both with smoking and drinking. I have never been used to cocktails and have always been frightened that I would "go under" sometime ..."

"This week I've been to XV club, out for tea and having friends for dinner and bridge tonight. Then Friday, Mrs. Perkins, Alpha Delta Pi, is in Kobe on her way to Peking so I'm having her up for dinner that evening. On Saturday, Professor and Mrs. Bartel of Iowa City are to be in Kobe, sightseeing after the world's engineering conference ... It will be so jolly to see them."

"Dear Earl, (Roberta's younger brother)
    ... I have a new pal - Helen Lamont, a new teacher at Kobe College who lives just two blocks away. We've been doing a lot of hiking in the mountains and have been out to see plum blossoms together. It is so fine in this land where there are so few telephones to have a person near enough to run down and ask to go somewhere with you ... Do write often Earl for I love your letters and you.
    Your sister, 'Berta"

NIKKO - TEMPLES and KEGON FALLS

... the friend who headquarters with us when in Japan announced at the breakfast table that she was ready to go on some trips here in Japan and proposed that I join her in a weekend at Nikko – the fare one way being my birthday present ... so after my last class in the late afternoon I boarded the III class express for Tokyo with her. We caught the next train and after another four hours were in the famous place.

There is a saying here "You cannot say Nikko (meaning splendid) until you have been to Nikko." In the mountains north of Tokyo are these famous temples built around the tombs of Ieyasu and Iemitsu – the latter being the first Tokugawa shogun. The hillsides are covered with tall cryptomeria trees and among them stand the temples, all painted a flaming red with magnificent carvings both inside the temples and out. The gates are the most interesting of all with ornate lacquer and gold doors, then above them elaborately carved flowers, figures and scenes.

There are two special things tourists remember about Nikko aside from the beauty of the whole place and they are the three monkeys and the sleeping cat. The latter is carved in a frieze above a door and though not particularly beautiful it is unique because the one armed carver did it. I have forgotten his name but all of his works are famous. "See no evil, hear no evil, speak no evil" - the three monkeys with hands over eyes, ears and mouth are found in every country I think but the original is here in Nikko ...

We reached Nikko at noon and went directly to the foreign hotel where we ordered practically everything on the menu, we were so hungry. Then after a tour through only one of the two temple grounds we decided to go on to Lake Chuzenji and spend the night ...

Chuzenji was 8 miles up in the mountains and we went part way by train and the latter half by bus on the controlled motor road, a series of twists and turns with deep precipices on either side. As we rode higher, the maple leaves grew more red and flaming until at the top the shores of the lake and Mt. Nantai was a mass of color. We spent the night in a Japanese inn and slept like tops all night.

Our plan was to walk back to Nikko from Chuzenji so as to enjoy the beauty of the mountains so you can imagine our disgust upon waking to find it raining . . .

— • —

As we ate breakfast we considered all sorts of plans and finally hit on this one. Shoes are almost as precious as gold itself and clothes too so we had the maid buy us each a pair of "tabi", the small white stockings that just come to the ankles, and a pair of "waraji", straw sandals. These we put on our feet and we turned up our coats, then got about five sheets of "aberagaue" an oiled wrapping paper, of which we made coats. One sheet we put over our hats and the rest we draped about ourselves until Lillian at least looked just like a sheik.

— • —

Nikko
October 1928

We sent our "furoshikis" down by bus and we started off to see the sights of Chuzenji and to walk down.

Kegon Falls is the most famous in Japan and is truly beautiful. From Lake Chuzenji a stream flows out making these falls and many smaller ones, finally flowing under the sacred red lacquer bridge at Nikko. Kegon Falls is unique in that aside from the main stream there are more than a dozen tributaries coming out of the rocks, joining the main stream at the bottom. This foaming stream dashing over the rocks in a setting of flaming maples was worth coming 18 hours on the train to see.

Kegon Falls descends 318' from Lake Chuzenji. It was created by the eruption of Mount Nantai 20,000 years ago.

Having made the trip to the Falls successfully in our footwear and paper coats we decided to walk the 4 miles down to Umagaeshi, thus enjoying the scenery for the prettiest part of the way. In spite of the rain it was a beautiful walk and though our feet got frightfully cold we enjoyed wading into every puddle and squashing the mud between our toes.

Luck was with us . . . we found a bus just leaving for Nikko. We kept on our peculiar garb and visited the second temple grounds . . . It was most amusing to see people turn from the temples to look at us and some foreign tourists whom we met couldn't hide their laughs. We explained however that we had come down from Chuzenji and then they envied us our trip.

From the temples to the station was about a mile so we walked down, stopping along the way to buy our "omiyage," a gift to give when returning. Nikko is famous for its peppermints so I bought a box for Grace as omiyage, then some "Yokan" for the servants and the girls at the Y. When I told the girls Friday that I was going to Nikko they all said bring us some "Yokan." You see you are just expected to bring back a present for each member of your household when you go away.

We reached the station in time for an earlier train than we expected . . . so we collected our baggage and then went to a tea house nearby and asked if they could make a bath for us. This they did and while the water was heating we had a Japanese lunch and dried some of our wet clothes over the charcoal fire. After a hot bath, and a change of clothing, we put on dry shoes and went to the train fresh as could be. This noon I will be back at work and 'twill be a busy week. Though I've done this whole trip III class and have spent two full nights on the train, I slept well."

Nikko Toshogu is a Shinto shrine built in 1617. The Pagoda is in front of the main entrance and is in memory of Tokugawa Ieyasu, founder of the Tokugawa Shogunate, which ruled Japan for over 250 years until 1868.

TWO FRIENDS AND MEN

"Jae dearest,
 Since I have two letters and a card from you to answer I have taken my machine in my lap and a roll of paper under my arm and perched myself on the "roka"of my room to write to you. It is a hot night and a few breezes do find their way up here from the sea and then there is a most gorgeous moon. Here I sit enjoying it all by myself. Isn't it pathetic??? Tiny white clouds are wafting by and the beams on the water are sparkling and dancing about in great glee. What fun it would be to have a canoe and and and - but I'm in Japan with no man within a hundred miles whom I know - really - with my best beloved many miles away . . ."

"I'm so glad you found Spike as fine as ever during your short visit in Chicago. How fortunate you are to see him even that little while. Ten minutes with Harvey might tell me everything but even that is denied this far away . . . No letter from Harvey today . . . but - cheer up—happier days are coming I keep telling myself . . . Harvey writes me almost every week . . ."

"Jae dear,
 I just get dizzy when I think of what to do when I get home . . . Even though I decide not to marry I'll not be coming back to Japan. I think the day of the foreign secretary in the YW in Japan is fast rolling by. I might be given an opportunity of going to some other country and that I should like."

"I've had few letters from Harvey this fall and I've written fewer . . . I'll just drift on until we can see each other and talk together . . . I do agree with you that a husband should have some social qualities, education, etc. That's one thing I like about Harvey. He is well read, talks interestingly, has traveled . . . but enough of that."

". . . Your lengthy letter was waiting for me when I got back to Kobe . . . What a fine time you did have in California . . . As for Win, it's a shame he wasn't as nice as his pin and couldn't stay next to your heart . . . I am at sea again and I'm just letting things ride as they are at the present . . . I"ll let you know when there is a change and do report to me, Jae, about your "next."

". . . Since Iowa beat Wisconsin I'll have something to crow about over Harvey. Incidentally a nice fat box of chocolates arrived from him this morning. I can't think of a thing to send him for Christmas but will have to scout about this next week . . ."

FASHION—HATS AND . . .

"Jae dear,

What are the new styles for spring? Are hats felt? etc. etc. etc. Do keep your "fur off" sister informed, won't you? I've got to get some new clothes soon – a hat, evening dress, afternoon dress - oh dear! My increase of $16.50 per month since January 1, 1929 will all have to go into clothes I fear. This raise came unexpectedly but it was welcome!!!!

". . .Thanks for offering to shop for me. How I long for some new clothes but have spent all my pennies on traveling this summer so I am clinging to my old duds. Unfortunately they are all wearing out so I'm sewing at present. I think I sent you a sample of my blue silk. I'm going downtown tomorrow and buy some Japanese kimono material and then Saturday sew up a dress for every day."

"Jae my dear,

. . . I must go to the tailor to have a darling evening dress which my sister sent out fixed. I was so desperate for clothes that I sent out an SOS and this lavender gorgette dress is the first answer to my call. It looks nice on me, I think, but the slip is too tight.

Wonder of wonders I matched the gorgette and slip so I think my tailor can fix me up. Peking is a gay city and as I have a friend in the British Legation there will probably be some parties. What fun."

"... as Lillian had been in Berlin she brought back some new clothes and one dress which didn't fit her well she gave me. It is a blue knitted silk - waist of cross stripes red and gray and skirt of plain blue. It is a pretty thing and very becoming. As I am quite desperate for clothes it was most welcome. Lillian always brings back pretty gifts to us but for this past year I've been forwarding her mail, getting her baggage through customs etc. etc. for her so I suppose that is why she showered me with such lovely things.

This is a beautiful day with the sun shining and warm.
With dearest love to you, Roberta"

"Jae my dear,
The stockings arrived yesterday, duty-free, and they are perfectly lovely . . . The shades are just what I want - the darker pair to go with two dark silk dresses - the lighter ones to wear with some evening and dinner things. Thanks heaps for bothering about them."

"Dear Ruth, (Roberta's older sister)
. . . We have had very cool weather all spring but on June 1 summer suddenly descended upon us and today the sun is blistering hot. Now we are all rushing to the tailor to have him finish up our hot weather clothes. From now on until September nothing but thin silks or rather voiles will be comfortable, and we are having most things made sleeveless. I've discovered a number of backless dresses on the streets but I don't fancy them. Are they really wearing them at home? My! how behind the times I'll be when I return."

SOME BOOKS and MOVIES of the 1920s

"Jae dear,

What a happy surprise I did receive on a rainy sticky hot examination morning this week - the package of books from you!

I had been studying "Takuhon" for days and that morning my alarm had gone off at six and I had studied two hours before breakfast so you can imagine I wasn't the most cheerful person eating my morning orange. And then came the mailman - what fun!

Though this is only Sunday and exams were over Friday noon I've read "The General's Ring" and the poems, and I'm starting in the "Hounds of Spring." I love having the books. Thanks just heaps and heaps.

Before Clare leaves I'm reading her "A Lincoln" by Carl Sandburg and enjoy it immensely. Of course you've seen it. I think his style of writing is exquisite - he's still the poet - and having lived in the middle west all my life practically I thoroughly appreciate the settings he has described for Lincoln. Now that school is over I'm spending a good bit of time reading."

". . . Have you read "Good Conscience" by Olav Dunn – a Norwegian writer? It's rather brutal in parts but awfully well done – then the plot is so different. I'm trying to wade through "Recent Gains in American Civilization" but though I'm halfway through the book I'm getting very little information. Harvey flatters me when he thinks I might enjoy it."

". . . Saw *Ben Hur* at the movies and also *40,000 Miles with Lindberg* - very good both of them."

NORTH to HOKKAIDO

"...Today we are at our last stop in Hokkaido, at a beautiful lake far off the beaten track. We had to ride an hour in an old bus through the mountains, then more than an hour in a funny motorboat that hauls mostly freight in order to reach this nice hotel on Lake Toya. There are few guests here and we have only Japanese food but the quiet and beauty of the place is restful. Our hotel is right on the beach so we've gone swimming twice today and have had the sea to ourselves. The food has been really good for we've had omelets, fish, sort of lake trout, and plenty of rice. We carried cocoa and coffee and some butter and jam with us most of the way but here they have no bread even. By now we get along much better on Japanese food.

One day we got a car at Sapporo and drove out into the country visiting a dairy farm where they make cheese, and also a sheep farm. At the dairy farm Mr. Suido had studied both in Denmark and the U.S. and he had 15 cows which he was milking; that day he was threshing with modern machinery and I saw two tractors in use. They had made their cheese for that day so we couldn't see the process but they served us baking powder bread, cheese, milk and apple pie for a lunch. Mrs. Suido was dressed in foreign clothes, had three children and was busy from morning till night as our farmers' wives are . . .

The government brought specialists in agriculture from various countries to Hokkaido. Dr. Clark, an Amherst man, opened Imperial University in Sapporo which now has three large schools, Medical, Agricultural and Engineering . . . The grounds of the University cover acres and the campus is really beautiful. Sapporo is called the city of elms as the streets are lined with the tall spreading trees, a variety that blooms.

Hokkaido has been so much like Iowa that I've almost been homesick. Sarah (from Iowa) and I kept saying "This is like Iowa" and "That is like Iowa" until the others began teasing us.

Sweet corn was first grown domestically in the 1900s when the farmland of Hokkaido was being developed. The climate was too cold for rice farming and sweet corn became the major island crop.

Noboribetsu Onsen was another interesting place for there were hot springs like Yellowstone . . . with the huge crater like place with pool after pool of bubbling sulphur water. It was boiling hot everywhere and even the banks of the pools and streams felt hot through our shoes. There were no geysers like "Old Faithful" but small springs everywhere. From all these springs the hotels take water for their baths . . .

From our hotel we had to walk about two blocks to the bath house which was built over the stream running from the hot spring. It was left in its natural form with rocks here and there - just a house built over it - and in the corner on a rock stood a god with candles burning in front of it. It seemed so strange to undress in our room, don the hotel kimono, and with soap and towel in hand walk down main street a couple of blocks to our bath. Such is Japan, however!

Another interesting place we stopped was at Shiraoi where more than 400 Ainu live. The Ainu are the aborigines of Japan and have been crowded farther and farther north and have inter-married too so they are almost extinct. They are larger in body than the Japanese, have round eyes, wear long hair and long beards.

We visited a house which is made of straw with wooden beams and a hardwood floor and the man of the house showed us his arrows for catching bear and his fishing things. They make a poison out of a weed and insert it in the arrow. This poison is so deadly that in 15 minutes after he is hit, the bear is dead.

These people worship the Fire God and each morning go through a ceremony of putting some wine into the fire as an offering to the god. The next god is the one for children, then the god of bears and fish (because they live by fishing and hunting). In the three hours between trains we could see all of the village but now we want to read a new book published about them . . .

Hazel and I have just had a financial reckoning and find that we have done this whole trip including the travelling by boat and train for seven yen a day ($3.50). We think that is pretty good."

The Ainu are the original indigenous people of Hokkaido. Various assimilation policies, e.g. banning the Ainu language and children given Japanese names and put in Japanese schools, eroded their identity and traditions. In 1899, they were declared "former Aborigines" indicating they were integrated into the Japanese population.

In 2008, however, the government passed a resolution recognizing the Ainu as indigenous people with their own language, religion and culture. Government records indicate there now may be only 25,000 Ainu living in Japan.

Y.W.C.A. FUND RAISING

"Tomorrow our club girls are giving a strawberry party - selling dishes of berries all afternoon and evening and also having a victrola concert - to raise money for sending girls to summer conference at Gotemba. Some of the girls are coming this evening to make cookies and candy to sell too . . . Our concert last week was a success. The Y.W.C.A. hall was filled to overflowing . . ."

The Y.W.C.A. Conference Grounds at Gotemba were used by "Y"s throughout Japan for programs and conferences. The grounds included an auditorium, a dining hall, cottages and dormitories.

Getting ready for a hike at Gotemba.

MORE FUND RAISING

"In November the Y.M.C.A. and the Y.W.C.A. held a joint bazaar. Bazaars in Japan are very different from the ones we have in the States. Ours was typical and consisted of many shops brought by merchants to sell everything from gas stoves to candy, and of many eating places. Entrance tickets were sold which included the price of an entertainment given both afternoons and evenings. The Y.W. naturally took charge of the different eating booths selling rice curry, many kinds of Japanese food, coffee, tea, sandwiches and cakes. My particular task was supplying sandwiches for the counter and in the two days we made four hundred packages, each package containing five sandwiches. The whole affair was on such a large scale and demanded so much work that the two organizations deserved all of the y1000 profit . . ."

Roberta's Sept 1926-March 1927 Report to Y.W.C.A.

"Dear Mother and Father,

Shortly before Christmas I was told that we were to have an old clothes sale very soon . . . Our members had brought in used kimono, haori and obi and they were displayed on tables or on hangers in one of our club rooms and many Japanese and foreigners came to buy. Kimono are very expensive and they last a long time for only the best materials are used in their finest ones, so women welcome the opportunity of exchanging them. The beautiful silk obi, yards long, were very attractive to foreigners so altogether many things were sold. The Y.W.C.A. received a commission for selling the things."

(A year later)

"We are recuperating from our Christmas sale of used kimono which we had last Saturday. It was a very poor sale netting us only 200 yen while last year we made over 500 yen. Our new location had a great deal to do with it I'm sure, also the fact that there was another sale the same day. Next year we hope to have it earlier . . ."

". . . Oh yes the "Y" is giving a movie next Saturday the 29th to help clear up our debt of $1000. We'll certainly welcome our vacation in August."

"At last another bazaar is over and on Friday and Saturday I served 800 cups of coffee and tea besides 450 cakes. I was so weary Friday night that I couldn't sleep."

"Last Saturday, March 1, we gave a Doll Festival in the Union Church Parlors to make money for the Y.W. and it was a success financially as well as a joy to all who saw the dancing done by little Japanese children before the display of dolls. I was in charge so felt a great burden off my shoulders when all the tea had been served, the dancers sent home by taxies, and the dolls for the display wrapped and packed in their proper boxes."

Unique Fund Raising Opportunity

"Dear Mother and Father,

... I think you will be interested in the latest thing I am having to do for the Association. I am teaching a Demonstration Cooking Class at present and one of the young girls in the class asked me the other day if I would go out to her home and teach her Mother, married sister and aunt cooking.

It is not usual for us to go out and teach as we have so much to do inside the building and Grace didn't approve at all but Shikami San, the Education secretary, and I thought we'd like to try it until vacation anyway, thus making a little extra money for the Association which is more than $1000 in debt at present.

So a day was arranged for and we were met at Mikage station (the family lives in a suburb of Kobe) and taken to a beautiful mansion (that is the only word to describe their home) and were led through a beautiful hall with marble seats into a foreign style drawing room filled with beautiful furniture but very badly arranged. There we had tea and met the family and talked over the plans. It was decided that we should come out twice a month and that besides teaching cooking they wanted me to help them arrange their foreign rooms, equip their kitchen and help them buy dishes etc. etc.

It seems that the father is an electrical engineer and is at present working on some experiments for the government and that he entertains in his beautiful home a great deal.

As is true in most wealthy Japanese families the husband has been abroad, has learned to like foreign food, and wants to entertain in his home foreign style. But the poor wife who has stayed in the background all her life knows nothing about foreign ways and is at a loss to know how to satisfy her husband. So the cooking teacher of the daughter is called in to take over the management of the house for foreign entertaining.

> From the 1600s until the late 1800s, the powerful shoguns kept Japan in isolation. The Meiji Period began in 1868 with a new emperor who opened the doors of Japan to the world. This transition continued into the 1920s.
>
> As a result, the request of this family reflected the fact that Japan wanted to play a major role in the West and businessmen wanted to become acquainted with and feel at home in Western culture.

On that first day we went into the kitchen and found that they had nearly everything that one could possibly need in preparing foreign meals and that they had their own ice plant and many electrical conveniences which they haven't the slightest idea how to use.

Then last Wednesday we went out for the first lesson. As it was the first time to work in their kitchen and as I didn't know how much cooking they knew, I planned to make only veal birds, coffee cake, French fried potatoes and strawberry ice cream, not a whole meal but something substantial which could be made for the father later and something sweet to satisfy the "sweet tooth" of the women. We all donned aprons, began the cooking, I doing very little, and so our lesson began. Before we had finished the father came home and came out to meet me.

I next discovered him in the dining room bringing out the family silver and dishes and showing the maids how to set the table. Later as the coffee cake and meat were baking in the electric oven and we were busy frying the potatoes I began to chuckle to myself as it was all so humorous. Here was I, with my interpreter, Shikami San, to help when necessary, my class of three women with the Mother of the family just looking on, seven maids standing about ready to jump should I just breathe a wish for a spoon or bowl, and the Father of the family in his beautiful silk kimono setting the table in the next room!!!

When the dinner, as such, was ready there had to be a lesson given on setting the table, arranging silver, etc. etc. That finished we all sat down to the table, Father and Mother at the head and foot, Mother protesting because she really shouldn't sit down sharing places with her husband. Then all seven maids began bringing in the dinner and I was asked to direct their serving. That continued throughout the meal as did the directing of which fork, spoon or knife should be used for each course, by the members of the family. As the meal progressed the father said everything was delicious but to please make more next time as his son-in-law and brother, the husbands of the two women in the class, would be home for dinner and they wanted to share in the instructions given. So next week we make dinner for nine.

It is really rather frightening when I think how much they expect me to know. Fortunately last time I was able to answer all the questions they asked with the exception of when and how to serve the wines. Being an American, I explained, I couldn't give him help on that score. He seemed very much interested in the fact that we have prohibition but said that he did like a little whiskey with his dinner.

After coffee served in the drawing room they sent us back to Kobe in a taxi as it was raining. It had been a most interesting afternoon and now we are looking forward to our next lesson. They are really a most delightful family and the Father is not as overbearing as many Japanese men so it is going to be a pleasure to be with them. But before next Wednesday I must plan a seven course dinner for them."

"...Yesterday we had our second lesson and we prepared a nine course dinner, had it properly served and eaten—much to the satisfaction of them all. Shikami San and I got there at 1:30 and left at 8:30 so we were both frightfully weary but it is a most interesting task. Our roast beef was delicious and the grape nut ice cream with chocolate sauce, whipped cream and cherries was the best I've eaten in Japan—delicious because we used real cream, something most households can't afford out here. Tomorrow I take Grace out to see what can be done to improve their foreign style drawing room. Grace is doing that part gratis but for the two lessons in cooking, each month the Association gets y50 ($25) so it's a fine revenue for the YW. Besides that they gave us y15 for carfare so we brought in y65 for this month.

Next time we will have pictures taken for the big brother is quite a photographer and it's an eventful day when they all prepare the foreign dinner. I didn't make anything yesterday, simply supervised the cooking done by my three pupils and their five maids, and felt a bit like I imagine Mother felt as I see her directing the Thanksgiving dinner at the church in olden days. And by the way they have turkeys and next fall want to learn how to roast them. Help!!!! Indeed I'll practice at home before that lesson!!

The young daughter had been on a trip to Miyajima this week so brought me some "omiyage." It was a damascene bracelet – a lovely thing with scenes of Miyajima on each link. Also a box of correspondence cards. While I'm probably giving them something of the foreign way of living, I'm also appreciating the fact that I can go into a Japanese household and be "taken in" enough to see how they live and I value the opportunity that has come . . ."

"My dear Mother,
. . . I've been having a nice time with the daughter of the family. I had the family in for tea last Wednesday and they came at two-thirty and stayed until six so guess they enjoyed themselves. Even the dear sedate Mother chatted and took in everything in the house, acted as at home and at ease that I was truly thrilled. She invited me to the daughter's wedding reception April 10 (the wedding will be at a Shinto shrine I imagine) and asked me to help her with her house furnishings, silver, dishes, etc.

On Monday then I met the daughter who came with her maid and we picked out several patterns of silver for her to take home and choose from. Then we looked at dishes and kitchen utensils, bought victrola records and just had a good time shopping until Shikami San could leave the "Y" and meet us . . . for lunch. When it was over I had to go to a graduating class party and give a speech so couldn't go to the movies with them but am looking forward to other shopping expeditions. It's such fun to buy for them for I need never think of how much money I can spend. They always want the best and are willing and can pay for it.

Of course they brought me gifts when they came for tea - a beautiful square for a cushion, writing paper and a lacquer candy bowl. I really am embarrassed at receiving so many things and I make no attempt to return them for I can't . . ."

"July 1929
Dear Mother and Father,
. . .This week I gave my last lesson before vacation. When Shikami San and I arrived we were taken into the daughter's room and while we drank some iced tea we were each presented with a gift. July is the Obon festival, a season when gifts are exchanged much like our Christmas time. Shikami San received material for a kimono and a part of an obi while I received four yards of gorgette for a dress, sample enclosed. Isn't it beautiful material? I took it immediately to my tailor and by getting two yards more he is making me a lovely dress with separate sleeves so I can wear it for either afternoon or evening.

After we had eaten our dinner that night they showed us the moving pictures they had taken last time with "yours truly" the movie star, walking in the garden, then preparing the dinner and eating with the family at the table. It was a queer sensation watching myself perform but I must admit it was an interesting movie.

When we left they asked how soon we could come again so they want to continue next fall too. As I go out only twice a month they prepare the menu over and over again during my absence, even inviting guests in for dinner as they are putting it all to practical use. Did I tell you in my last letter that the father was called to Tokyo on government business due to the change of ministry but delayed his trip one day so as not to miss the dinner. I think that quite a compliment, don't you?

With much love, your daughter, Roberta"

CHANGING TIMES for AMERICANS in the JAPANESE Y.W.C.A.

". . . Last weekend we had a conference of foreign secretaries in Tokyo and we all had to go . . . Our meetings were held at the new Tokyo YW building that opened this month. . . . It was the first time during my stay in Japan that we have gotten together as a group of foreigners and it was fun for the 19 of us to be together. So many girls are going home this year and new people are not coming out so our number is dwindling."

"My dear Mother and Father,

. . .When Grace returned yesterday she told me that the time had come for going home, she thought, and that she had booked passage for the latter part of October. Imagine what a blow!!! We all came out here, you know, on contract but with the understanding that when your particular piece of work was done we should leave. As general secretary in Kobe she feels that the executive work should be in Japanese hands and that now is the time for it to be done so her resignation goes to the Board of Directors next Monday. While I feel she is doing the right thing and agree with her absolutely, it leaves me the only foreigner on the Kobe staff and rather alone in the world. Though the administration should be and will be entirely Japanese in Kobe now, there is still work for me to do in training secretaries to do club work, so I must stay on for a while at least, if under the new regime I'm able to continue my work. Then this being a port city there is a place for one secretary to be on hand as far as tourists and contacts with foreigners are concerned.

During this past year there has been a great exodus of YW secretaries and we've all been saying that in the near future there would be only one foreigner, then no foreigners in the centers but I didn't dream that I'd be the first one foreigner left alone in a city. As it is I am going to make the best of it and it is very possible that if I can exercise enough patience, it will all be for the best for the association . . .

At Gotemba I'll have to go over the matter of living arrangements with Miss Scott but . . . she wants me to keep the house and get someone to live with me. I must do a certain amount of entertaining and it's expensive to live anywhere so I agree that to keep the house is the only thing to do. It rather frightens me when I think of maintaining a house alone and the burden of things that will fall on me at the association but - I've been in Kobe three years now and have many friends - and I feel that we are doing the right thing . . . I'm going to face the year with all the faith and courage I can muster . . . and I really have high hopes for the year."

"We had a Secretaries' conference at Gotemba last week with forty-three of us there. Though a majority of the Japanese staff (there were only twelve of us foreigners) were very young, they looked mighty promising for the future of the Association."

Roberta was invited to a "Moon Viewing" dinner in Kobe.

"Moon Viewing" time comes at the full moon in September and is a time for making offerings of thanks to the moon.

After dinner . . . we all went a little way into the mountains where we could look over the whole city of Kobe which was beautiful lighted and watched the moon.

On July 7 is "Tanabata" when thanks are offered to the stars and on January 5 when an offering is made to the sun."

PEKING (Beijing)
SUMMER PALACE, MING TOMBS
and the GREAT WALL

"August 3, 1929
My dear Mother and Father,
 Greetings from IIIrd class of the *Choko Maru* somewhere on the high seas off the coast of Korea which is in view at the time of writing! We left Kobe at noon August first and had a beautiful trip through the Inland Sea sailing in between the many islands . . . and now we are in the open sea headed for Tientsin.
 Grace, Miss Scott and Anne Topping, a friend of mine, are traveling first class as are many other people whom we know so we are having visitors down here all the time. As we can't go up they must come see us so it really looks as if we are very popular.
 Our IIIrd class quarters consist of long rows of tatami matting on which men, women and children sleep side-by-side, but we have our space filled with baggage and simply live out on deck in the chairs we brought with us. They are the canvas folding kind and we can make them high for sitting or low for sleeping. We rented blankets and simply don't undress - just sleep out on deck under the stars - a wonderful feeling. Our chairs are very comfortable and so easily moved that we can follow the shade and keep cool. It seems strange to be wearing a coat today after sweltering in the heat of Kobe for two months.
 For IIIrd class we have Japanese food but we brought our own. After sandwiches the first day we've enjoyed crackers, cheese, sardines, tea, coffee and lots of fruit. We have our meal on deck too, the stewards always bringing us two cups and a pot of hot water. When we run out of food we can order meals down from first class but we are faring very nicely.

Of course our deck isn't sheltered so if it rains I don't know what we'll do as it's stifling hot down below. We may take our chairs up to the first class deck and I'm sure they won't put us out. The trip is taking us from Thursday noon till early Monday morning, then six hours on the train from Tientsin to Peking . . . Our trip from Kobe to Peking is costing us $12.30. Can you imagine it?

I'm so glad to be having vacation for though I enjoyed my swimming classes at the cottage during July they were very strenuous. As I slept on the floor and usually with a room full of girls, I didn't get my proper rest and then the long car rides back-and-forth were hard too. I left my swimming suit at home but I'm carrying with me the brownest tan I've ever had. My face is red from the wind today but my arms and shoulders have been so burned that the sun can't hurt them anymore. I certainly am a sight!!!

Before leaving Kobe I had to go out to "play" one day.
(To see the family for whom Roberta was teaching cooking)

I wore the dress they gave me and of course they were terribly pleased. I must buy presents for them all in Peking to bring back with me.

The boat is beginning to roll so badly I'd better "lie low" or I'll be ill. I'll write again from Peking.

Much love always,
Roberta

Had a storm last night but we moved our chairs up to first class deck and slept well though we missed the stars. Our friends have been down to call, several of them this morning, and one brought us delicious melons so we've had plenty of fruit today . . ."

"My dear Mother and Father,

Our third day in this old historic city is drawing to a close and I have not put down on paper any of the happenings. Instead of writing in my diary this trip I'm writing a journal to you which I'd appreciate your keeping for me. Earl might make copies and send on to the rest of the family if you think they'd like to hear of my wanderings

After an uneventful boat trip of four days from Kobe we landed near Tientsin on our scheduled time but in a downpour of rain. As we put our baggage through customs and fought with the coolies to carry it to the train, put it on, and then to get our tickets, we became drenched - hats, dresses and shoes dripping with water but our spirits were still high as we rode through the flooded country five hours to Peking.

We had wired the Language School Hostel where we had engaged rooms that we would arrive at seven and as I was the one who had written, the coolie gave the card to me and I had to direct our party of six through customs again, get bags and self into rickshaws and our caravan off to the school.

They had sent the coolies from the school and one boy who spoke English attached himself to me and asked me to have him during my stay, which I am doing. His name is Shee and he is young and a good runner so on all our tours we lead the party. When we go into shops, he is at my elbow, helps me count my money to see I'm not cheated, carries my parcels and is spoiling me in any number of ways. But I'm ahead of my story. The ride from the station took a half hour and we were tourists for sure as we gazed from left to right not wanting to miss any of the strange sights of the city."

THE SUMMER PALACE

"At the school I found a note from Mac saying that he had come down from Dairen where he was on business and would have tomorrow for sightseeing. So he came out for me early the next morning and we had a busy but happy day. Everyone agreed that with only one day here, the Summer Palace should be visited so we got a hamper of lunch from his hotel, a taxi, and took my coolie along as interpreter and off we went seven miles out of the city to the summer resort of the Emperors for the last three centuries. Due to the disturbances within and without China, the ruling family was not able to go far from Peking so this palace was used the most, hence most beautifully decorated.

It was noon when we reached the outer wall so we sat in the car and ate our lunch, then began the delightful tour through the gardens, courtyards and temples which surrounded the palace. The palace was occupied until 1909 and when the Imperial family left in haste, the doors were locked, and the rooms now can be seen by looking through broken panes and torn away paper from the windows and they are just as they were left. There are inches of dust on everything and the pictures, paintings and treasures are not displayed to advantage at all.

The buildings themselves however are gorgeous. The marble gates, the bronze temples, the highly colored tile roofs and the long galleries facing on the lotus pond filled with lilies make the site one of the most beautiful in Peking. From one of the temples high up on the hillside we looked out over the pond with the camel back bridges and on to the Western hills beyond - a sight most gorgeous after recent rains . . ."

THE MING TOMBS

> The Ming Tombs are the mausoleums of 13 of the 16 emperors of the Ming Dynasty, 1368-1644, in a valley with a river and surrounded by mountains.

". . . Every visitor to Peking must go to the Great Wall and also see the Ming Tombs so a party of eight of us decided we'd combine the two and make the trip in two days. Last Friday morning we rose early, donned our knickers and tied up four lunches apiece in "furoshikis" and started off to the station to take the 7:40 train to Nankow. We took Shee, my rickshaw coolie, with us to buy tickets and be our interpreter as he knows some English so he carried our basket containing four bottles of water. Our train pulled in on time and we scrambled into the boxcar with all the soldiers and coolies travelling in that direction and chose the doorway so some of us at least could let our legs dangle and thus be comfortable.

It was a beautiful morning, the car wasn't too crowded and we were in good spirits so we didn't mind sitting on the dirty floor for the two hour ride. When we got off the train at Nankow we were glad we had Shee with us for the men with donkeys to ride to the Ming Tombs simply swarmed about and tried to lift us onto their donkeys and they were such dreadful looking characters that it nearly frightened us. Shee, however, bargained with them to take us the ten miles to the Tombs and to spend the night wherever we chose. We discovered the foreign hotel was closed and there were only two beds in the Chinese inn which wasn't at all inviting anyway.

So off we started - eight of us and Shee on donkeys with five men walking beside us. I had chosen a tall donkey because the stirrup straps seemed longer but when one girl was thrown off as her donkey stumbled, I began to wish I had taken a tiny animal. However, my "steed" proved to be quite sure footed and though

Marble archway built in 1541 which marked the lane to the Tombs.

he insisted on going over the steepest precipice every time, I clung valiantly on. After finding a stream and riding for an hour through corn fields, rocky river beds and lanes we at last came to the Pailon, an archway which marked the lane to the Tombs. There we sat to admire the delicate carvings and beautiful lines and to rest. We could have consumed every drop of water in the bottles then and there but we didn't know where we could get another supply so we restrained ourselves and soon started on for the last two hours of riding and walking.

These tombs were built before Columbus discovered America - around 1424 I think - so we weren't at all surprised to find the road gully washed even deeper by the recent rains. We trudged on and rode occasionally and soon came to the marble animals which guard the pathway and are a substitute for the attendants of older days who were buried with the Emperor. There were dogs both kneeling and standing, elephants, camels, horses and several men - all twice or three times life-size - really very well done in marble. Farther on we welcomed the chance to shed shoes and hose and wade across a river which had to be forded.

I think the sun was never so hot as that afternoon and walking over the hot sand we thought that the warm beach would be an ideal place to spend the night. But first, though almost overcome by the heat, we went on to the Tomb of the Emperor Yung-Lo, the nearest of the 13 tombs (the last of the purely Chinese dynasty) within a several mile radius. The tomb itself is enclosed within a high wall with sacrificial altars, the Buddhist temple and the burial tablets. In the courtyard are many silver bark pine trees which are found in Peking only and they say are associated with burial places. I forgot to mention that along the pathway there is the oldest tomb in China, the stone being the tablet on the back of the turtle.

Before we paid proper respect to the Emperor buried there we tried to regain our equilibrium by drinking cup after cup of boiling water. Truly I've never suffered so from heat as I did that afternoon. But the hot water seemed to quench our thirst and revive our spirits so that we could appreciate what we'd made such a journey to see.

The path to the tombs is a four mile lane, The Sacred Way, bordered by 36 huge stone human and animal sculptures.

We had our bottles filled with water, got an extra can of hot water (a standard oil can) and started back to the stream which we had forded to make the remnant of an old marble bridge there our camping grounds for the night. But the first thing we did was to go in for a swim in the clear, cool water. And did it feel good? It put new life into all of us and we even enjoyed the sandwiches of our lunches which had been jostled about on the backs of the donkeys in the sweltering heat all day.

It was gorgeous moonlight - almost full moon so there was no darkness and at eight o'clock we had buried ourselves in sand, eight of us in a row, Shee and a donkey man not so far away. But we soon discovered that the sand was damp and with no blankets and not even sweaters or a single wrap, the marble slabs of the bridge heated by the sun proved more comfortable in spite of its hardness. I had an air pillow with me and was really quite comfortable until a cool breeze came up which drove us off our warm beds to the shelter of the bridge itself underneath on some rocks. There after trying all the rocks away from the wind we decided to sit up till morning. The moon was almost bright enough to read by and the stars were beautiful so we studied the heavens, told stories, took exercises and tried to amuse ourselves till daybreak.

We had one fright in the night though when we saw two figures emerge from the other side of the bridge and come towards us. They had poles over their shoulders and baskets on each side but were dressed in rags so looked ghostly at night. When they saw us they stopped in their tracks and we stood up not knowing what to do when the faithful Shee called to them and they went on past us over to him where they stopped and chatted for an hour or so. We decided they were probably farmers carrying their products into town in the cool of the night.

THE GREAT WALL

We had asked the donkey men to be ready to start at four AM so that we could catch a seven o'clock train for the "Wall" and we were surprised to find it not yet daylight when they came up for us. However we started on, picking our way in the semi-darkness for, tho' the moon had gone down, the stars were still bright. It was so cool and we had gotten so chilled that we walked nearly all of the ten miles back, reaching the station just in time to jump into a coal car which was the "train" going to the "Wall."

It was just an hour's ride so we didn't mind having no chairs and we stood at the two windows looking at the beautiful mountains on both sides with the Wall or rather parts of it visible at numerous places. From the station we climbed twenty minutes and reached the Wall itself, sat in the old watch towers and looked off to Mongolia with the donkey and camel trains along the winding path through the pass.

The Great Wall

> The Great Wall is about 2700 years old, constructed as a military defense to resist invasionss from nomadic tribes of the north, and was built off and on between 475-211 BC and 1644-1911. Guards at the beacon towers could see invaders and with smoke signals or gunshots warn guards in other towers. The wall is an average height of 20-30', average width of 21.3' and is 13,170 miles long.

We got another train back at twelve, boxcar type simply packed full with men, women, babies, bundles, coal, fur coats and what not and hot as !!!!! We truly thought we'd not survive the four hour ride back to Peking. We were all so sleepy after our night up that we didn't dare sit in the doorway for fear of falling asleep and falling out. The smells of the car, the coal dust and desert sand that sifted in, and the weariness of our bodies made the trip seem endless but at four we arrived at the station, got taxis back to the school, took baths, and I for one was in bed at five and didn't waken till seven the next morning.

I had a bit of a cold when I woke up and had I stayed in all day I'd been fine but for two weeks I'd had an engagement for a picnic at the Jade Fountain, ten miles out in the Western Hills beyond the Summer Palace and of course I had to go. It was a delightful trip and we had a delicious lunch which we ate by the pool of jade green spring water, bubbling all the time - the source of the stream that leads from the Summer Palace on down to the Forbidden City in Peking. The ride through the country was beautiful and restful but when we returned about five I had to dash into other clothes and go out to a tea. My voice was about gone by that time and after I'd entertained a friend all evening sitting in the garden I was unable to say good night and today I've gone about whispering. By tomorrow I should be well for I'm feeling fine . . .

I have not told half of my doings here but think I'd better get this in the mail . . .   Dearest love, Roberta"

CELEBRATIONS

EASTER

"... Then came Easter Sunday. The YM and the YW here always have a sunrise service at Suwayama, the mountain at our back door, and we all got up for it at 6 o'clock ... While the service was all in Japanese, it was an inspiration to see the 450 Japanese who had come out for it ... "

CHRISTMAS

"Dear Mother and Father,

Were I a writer I would tell the tale of the Christmas tree which now stands in our living room. There are nine darling youngsters in my English class and I had them (and their mothers) come here for Christmas ... The children had great fun putting on the tinsel and silver stars. We sang songs we had learned and had cocoa and cookies. Then I took off the trimmings and sent the tree to the Y.W.C.A. building by a rickshaw man for a Business Girls Club banquet. Next day it stayed there for a Girl Reserve pageant. Then we took it to the Methodist Church for our Association Christmas."

Following is a summary of the tree's further travels: Roberta went with Kawamoto San to her Sunday school for 100 children at the Kanebo factory, trimmed the tree, all sang songs and each child received an arm full of oranges. Then one of the factory men helped Roberta carry it back to their house for the staff Christmas party.

Next Roberta and Kawamoto San took the 7' tree on the street car to Nagata, the slum section of Kobe, for the Friday night school for youngsters. At the car stop, one of the boys swung the tree over his shoulders and paraded down the street to a Christmas progam for 150 childen and gifts of oranges. The tree, untrimmed for the sixth time, was taken by Roberta on the streetcar to her house for Christmas Day supper with the Y secretaries.

THE NEW YEAR - 1928
Since the Emperor died in December 1926,
the year 1927 had been a year of mourning.

"Dear Mother and Father,
New Year's was very thrilling this year because the Imperial mourning of last December made all celebrating out of the question then. I was most interested in seeing the decorations . . . before the gates of homes, the stalks of bamboo cut flute shapes together with pine branches and a sort of leaf peony . . . and above the doors a wreath of rice straw with a lobster and an orange in the center. Even on the door of the humblest home we saw at least a sprig of pine to show it was New Year's."

Traditional New Year Poetry Game
"Yoshia San, our maid, has often wanted to teach the Poetry Game they play on New Year's Day so this afternoon we had a party - inviting girls from her class at night school.

This game consists of a reader reading the short poems - 100 of them - and the players having them all before them on the floor and quickly pulling out the matching card. We were six playing, three on each side but Ethel and I used only four or five cards while the others each had twenty some - that was all we could remember. The girl who read used sort of a sing song voice - they are taught to read it like that in school and it was really lovely. Just for fun Ethel and I dressed up in kimono too so we could sit nicer on the floor and it tickled the girls to see us. We served foreign tea and cakes and candy and one girl who played the piano very well gave us a concert. It was such a nice way to begin the New Year."

GRADUATION DAY
JAPANESE LANGUAGE CLASS
Roberta received her first and second year diplomas
and played the role of Joseph in the play.

"June 30, 1929
Dear Mother and Father,

    This is eleven o'clock in the morning so you know this is the beginning of vacation, else I couldn't be writing a letter at this time. I feel I haven't written a decent letter to you for ages so I am taking this morning to catch up in my correspondence with you.

    I went into seclusion again for some time before exams but now that they are a thing of the past I feel better about them. The enclosed copy of one set of questions will show you why I dreaded them. You can see how we can play a little game with ourselves as we walk along the street trying to make out the characters on the store signs but when you must know the exact reading and not just the meaning alone in an examination it is a different matter.

    I am enclosing a program of our Graduation Day exercises. We students did everything with the exception of the speech by a member of the School Committee . . . The play of course took the most time. I had costumes and properties from the Y.W. and from the house and that took time besides learning my lines.

    Joseph was a very talkative chap I decided when I began learning my lines, and I do wish the Pharaoh hadn't had such a long dream for I had so much interpreting to do. The hardest part of it all were the changes in my speeches. As a young boy I used very respectful language to my elder brothers and father, then when interpreting Pharaoh's dream I used polite, court language.

Of course when my brothers came to buy corn I was most impolite to them and used coarse men's language but in the same act, when revealing myself, I changed back to polite speech. All that meant that I never could make up a line if I missed it for I would have said it in women's language which would never do, being a man.

Everything went all right, even my one speech that was one type written page long, until my very last speech when in the last line I told my brothers to hurry home and bring our dear father "Jacobu" out to me and I made a funny mistake which set the audience roaring.

I thought at the time that they were amused at Joseph embracing Benjamin (the Y.W. falling into the arms of the Anglican clergy) but I found out later that I had said "Chichi ue wo koko ni motte kite ku da sai" instead of "chichi ue wo koko ni tsurete kite ku da sai." They both mean to bring, but "motte" is used in bringing a package or something like that which is distinctly carried in the hands or arms, while "tsurete" means to lead a person or take a person.

The secretaries at the Y all greeted me with "motte kite ku da sai" when I next appeared and they love teasing me about it but I don't mind. After the program was finished we had loads of ice cream to eat and then went home happy to be free again.

Your daughter, Roberta"

IKEBANA - The Art of Flower Arrangement

"Dear Mother and Father,

...You ask about flower arrangement lessons. Yes, we each pay for our own flowers and they usually come out to twenty-five cents each time. Flowers are abundant all the year in Japan and even on the coldest days we see flower women going down the streets selling their baskets of flowers. Soon we will be seeing men sitting on the street corners selling rose plants for about 20 or 30 cents a plant. Japan is certainly the land of flowers. We have cut ones on our table all the time and in our rooms, too. With Clare and me both taking flower arrangement lessons we have our house full most of the time."

Flower Arrangement Class - Roberta is at far right.

"Yesterday I had a delightful time being entertained by my Japanese friend. At nine I went to her house to see her flower arrangements. She is in my cooking class . . . She explained her arrangements and then we had tea, cakes and candy . . . I do so enjoy visting my Japanese friends!"

" My teacher speaks no English at all and is very Japanese in all her ways so I am learning more than flowers from her each lesson."

"Dear Midge, (Roberta's sister-in-law)
We are having Flower Arrangement lessons each Wednesday . . . One can study years and years, you know, but I'm beginning to "feel" how the arrangement should be now."

CHANOYU - The Tea Ceremony

". . . Ceremonial tea is served by most of the upper class women when you call for special occasions . . . So many of my friends serve it to me when I am entertained there that I am awfully glad to know just how to drink it, what to say, etc. etc. It is a long process and most people who do it well have studied for ten years so I shall never do it perfectly . . ."

From Roberta's 1928 diary, March 1:
"Our flower arrangement teacher took three of us to have Tea Ceremony in a tea house. She told us just what to do, to go up and admire the fire box, the water bowl and then return. We tried to drink tea according to our lessons but it was difficult to remember it all."

> The tea ceremony has its roots in Zen Buddhism and the ritual, as practiced in the 1900s, evolved in the sixteenth century. Powdered green tea, Matcha, is used and the ceremony follows a ritual which represents harmony, respect, purity and tranquility.

HIKING AROUND FUJI SAN and to MINOBU SAN

"Dear Mother and Father,

Last Monday was a holiday here for the Emperor offered the first rice of the season to the Gods - really a Japanese Thanksgiving Day. Twas rather convenient to have vacation on a Monday for it gave us a long weekend to do things.

On the Thursday before, a letter came from Gibbie saying that a group from Tokyo was planning to walk around Fuji San and the Shoji Lakes and asking that I join the party. Without hesitation I sent a wire saying "yes" and the next morning boarded the third class express for Tokyo . . .

Saturday

Though we had spent most of the night before chatting and drinking coffee (when this Swede and the Irish Gibbie meet it always happens), we felt fresh and gay as we boarded the 8:13 train at Idabashi and rode on the third class train for three hours to Otsuki where we chartered a bus, we were eight of us, and started for Yoshida. The ride through the country was glorious, the rice fields ready for harvest, the buckwheat in bloom, and cosmos growing as tall as I, and dahlias in the most gorgeous shades giving the villages a festive air. As we rode on farther into the mountains, the air became cooler and here and there we saw a flaming maple tree though it was too early for much color . . .

Lake Kawaguchi

It was after twelve when we reached Yoshida on Lake Kawaguchi, the second of the five lakes at the foot of Fuji San. (We had passed one.) Here we stopped at a teahouse and bought some hot tea and hot water to make our G. Washington coffee to drink with the sandwiches we had brought with us. It was bitter cold as we ate our lunch so we each got into our knapsacks and put on an extra pair of hose and pulled on a sweater under our jackets so as to keep warm on our half hour boat ride crossing this lake. Much to our dismay, however, as we got on our way, the sun sent out such warm rays that we wished for umbrellas rather than sweaters. At the opposite shore we began our hiking, shedding coats and tying them as well as "furoshikis" and packs on our backs.

Our path led us through a long tunnel and through some quaint villages, but very suddenly we came upon the third lake of the series. As it was the middle of the afternoon and there were still many miles to go, we took a launch across this lake too and then began a hike up about three ri (one ri is approximately two and one half miles) to the Fuji Hotel on Lake Shoji where we hoped to spend the night.

Lake Shoji and the Fuji Hotel

We found a good road . . . over dark lava beds with strange formations of ashen colored boulders with moss and pine trees all around us . . . We soon reached Lake Shoji but found that our hotel was another ri around the other side. There happened to be a man from the hotel there, however, who relieved us of our packs and took orders for our baths and a "guynabe" supper so we were able to strike off again into the woods which circled this lake and walk to the hotel.

As we reached the other side of the lake, the shadows were growing long and we hurried to an open space where we caught a magnificent view of Fuji San in the glow of the setting sun. For a few minutes the clouds wandered away, leaving the snow-covered crater of our sacred mountain reflecting the colors that changed from pinks to bluish lavenders and then a gleaming white as the sky grew darker. Oh! What a sight! Just to have had that one view of Fuji San was enough to last a long while.

Roberta is the hiker 2nd from the right.

At a Japanese inn the first ceremony is to drink a bit of tea and then don the kimono provided and afterwards enter the bath. As we were the only guests we had the bath to ourselves and also very good service - our charcoal stoves and all the preparations for our "guynabe" were in our room when we returned.

I can tell you it took only a short while to have our onions cooked, then add the mushrooms, cabbage, other vegetables and beef steak, all flavored with the sugar and "shoyu", then dish out our rice and put this mixture on top of it. We scarcely waited for our beaten eggs which, if the hot meat mixture is just dropped into the egg for a minute and then eaten, is delicious. I know I ate four bowls of rice and I think we all thought this was the best "guy-nabe" ever. We finished up with some Van Houten's cocoa which is easily carried and delicious just made in the cup.

As our beds were already made up on the floor in another room, we literally "crawled in as we were" not even removing our heavy kimono. Japanese bedding, as I think I have described before, consists of a heavy comforter on the floor and another equally heavy one to cover yourself with. This latter does not tuck in around the neck so it's almost necessary to also wear a sweater or a kimono. It certainly did not take us long to get to sleep that night.

Sunday

We were awakened early the next morning by a downpour of rain so turned over and slept until eight o'clock but then found it had calmed down to a drizzle so off we started. We had found our baggage rather too much the day before so we hired a man to carry it for us this day as we had about six or seven ri ahead of us and all of that walking. We began climbing immediately upon leaving the hotel and for over an hour we hiked steadily upward. When we finally reached Panorama Hill we were dreadfully disappointed to find a heavy mist and rain which completely cut off our view of Fuji San.

From this point our journey was for the most part down hill . . . The villages and temples all along the way were very quaint and at one place we stopped to see some corn being pounded by the power from a water wheel. There are many mountain streams here and everywhere through the country districts you find these old fashioned wheels turning and squeaking but saving a great deal of hand power. By noon we had gone about eight miles so welcomed the box of sandwiches we had made that morning.

We stopped in a little village and found the best place for our picnic to be on the rocks in a tiny stream which ran through the town. Our carrier rustled up a little charcoal stove and a sauce pan so we made hot cocoa to eat with our sandwiches and the persimmons we bought off some trees nearby.

Naturally eight knicker clad women walking through a country village in Japan would cause commotion but when we talked Japanese, and then began cooking on a "hibachi," we had all the children in the neighborhood there watching us. They were very cunning though and soon became friendly, bringing us flowers, one by one.

Before we had finished our lunch the rain began to gently fall again so we packed up and donned raincoats and started off for Minobu San . . . We weren't certain just how far it was to this sacred mountain, and everyone whom we asked said from one to five ri, each with a different version, so we headed for the FujiKawa River hoping to ferry across before dark and then see where we could spend the night. After four more hours of hiking we were getting a bit weary when we saw signs of civilization and reached Shimo FujiKawa and the ferry. This river has a very swift current and the ferry was a clever arrangement whereby the boat was swung into the current and swung across.

By the descriptions given us, we thought we could get a bus just across the river for Minobu San but instead there was more than a mile to walk to the next village. At last we reached there only to find the last bus had gone. Since we were a large number, the shopkeeper agreed to call a special one for us but we had to wait a half hour for it to come back.

During that time we sat in his shop and sang English and Japanese songs until we had all the village folk about us. They all bowed us into the bus when we departed and soon we had covered a good many more miles and were at Minobu San, a mountain sacred to the Nichiren sect of Buddhism.

MINOBU SAN

Again we had a Japanese dinner, hot baths and beds on the floor. We were mighty willing to go to bed but after our hot baths we all felt really refreshed, and not as tired as we thought seventeen and a half miles of walking would make us. It was the longest hike I have ever taken but didn't mind it a bit. Just as we were getting into bed with the assistance of seven hotel servants (foreigners visit there so seldom they are a curiosity), they asked if we wanted to go to the service in the temple at five o'clock. Since they insisted it was the thing to do we had them call us at four-thirty the next morning.

Monday

It was at Minobu San that Nichiren, the founder of the sect, lived and spent his last days. He was an advanced thinker for his time and though exiled a number of times he was given permission to go back there and die. The temples are on the top of a mountain as usual but after the long climb we found ourselves in a beautiful temple court and were ushered into a service which the priests have each morning at that hour.

Temple at the top of the mountain

After they had chanted their service and left, one priest gave a short sermon which we stayed for and later were able to see the ceremony of opening the holy of holies where the figure of Nichiren is seated. An offering is made to him with a great deal of chanting and bowing and then the doors are closed again. We followed the crowd then and found ourselves in a separate room beautifully carved and colored with highly polished floors in the center of which is a glass jar in which are found the bones and ashes of Nicherin. Another ceremony was held here and then we returned to the hotel.

Just crossing FujiKawa the day before noting the swift current made us all wish for a boat to shoot the rapids . . . after much persistence and begging we finally persuaded some men to take us at least to the next train stop in their boat. They had come down the river carrying empty Red Crown Oil cans so they left a few for us to sit on and away we went with the current in the mountain river between beautiful hills. It was my first experience with rapids and now I'm wanting to go again.

At Toshima we got the next electric tram . . . and rode as far as Fuji. There we transferred to a train which took the Tokyo folks back home and Lillian and me to Numazu where we waited three hours for a third class train to get us back to Kobe in time for school in the morning. We spent our time in a very good restaurant we found in this tiny place and ate to our hearts' content. Our knickers were convenient wearing apparel for curling up in third class seats for the night so we really slept and felt quite fresh in the morning.

Of all the things I've done in Japan I think I enjoyed this the most of all. Such a trip in the states would be so expensive it would be prohibitive but even including my fare to Tokyo and back, 14 hours each way, I spent less than twenty dollars."

TEACHING SWIMMING

"Dear Mother and Father,

. . . Our cottage is just lovely and now that we have a nice woman staying there we can go out with our girls, stay overnight and have a good time without too much responsibility. I certainly am learning to live Japanese style for I sleep on the floor, eat on the floor and have Japanese food. It's great fun really!"

". . . It's nine-thirty Monday morning and I've given a swimming lesson (6:30 am), had breakfast, and done some sewing already. I'm out at our Suma cottage where I'm giving some courses in swimming and I'm practically living here. Usually I have to dash into my clothes and hurry back to the building for a nine o'clock class but today is holiday for the girls in DaiMaru department store so they come out here for swimming lessons . . . The DaiMaru girls began coming at ten and tho' I didn't go into the water until one I stayed till four and got frightfully burned.

My face, neck, shoulders and arms are aflame and I've been in agony all day. However with another greasing tonight I should feel better tomorrow and then in a day or so I'll begin to peel!!! Oh, how awful I look!"

"Dear Father,

This is such a hot afternoon we are about melting away. I must go out to the cottage for a swimming lesson at 6:30 but as a storm is coming up I'm afraid the waves will be too high to do any teaching. They were trifle last evening so I wouldn't let the girls stay in more than five minutes.

This morning the water was much nicer but I had 14 girls in the class which is a bit too many. I can't really teach them any and it's hard to keep track of them in the water so I think I'll divide them. I guess I told you that this group meets at 6:30 to 7:30 AM .

. . . Next week besides my swimming classes morning and evening I'm to teach a three day course in summer cooking from 10 to 1 all of us eating together the salad, sandwiches, cold drink and ice cream which I will demonstrate . . .

      Heaps of love, Roberta"

"Dear Mother and Father,

 I'm thoroughly enjoying the experience of sleeping on the floor every night, eating Japanese food (breakfasts such as cucumber soup and rice), and going to the public bath with the girls. Shikami San and Terada San, two secretaries, are in my swimming class so they spend the night here and of course we talk about everything under the sun as we lie in a row on the floor. I am certainly getting to know Japanese life this way. Of course they are so interested in my way of doing things too and the other day Shikami San asked me if I didn't have to wear suspenders to keep my stockings up. In turn I am learning how Japanese people dress so it's all mutual."

"My dearest Mother and Father,

 Tomorrow I start my day with teaching swimming at our summer camp at 6 AM. This year we were unable to find such a nice cottage and I don't care to stay overnight but just go out before class. This means that I get out of bed at 5 AM and have a forty minute street car ride before getting in to the water.

 Fifteen girls have registered so I will have a busy hour. It is such a trying time for we swim in the sea without the boundaries of a pool and I am constantly counting heads when not counting strokes. Usually around six the tide has gone out and the water is smooth so we can make progress."

Swimming and a "A Boston Tea Party"
Roberta and friends during a trip to Lake Nojiri

"Jae my dear,

    The last days in Nojiri were as full of fun as ever, swimming across the lake one day, bridge parties and one day a Boston Tea Party.

    Mrs. Shaw, who lives on the shore, invited twelve of us for luncheon and bridge so that we might watch the sailboat races. The boats started before we had been served coffee, so Mrs. Shaw served it to us on the pier. By some accident, the tea table was pushed an inch and the legs went into a crack in the pier and the dishes, cups, saucers, spoons and cream and sugar - everything slid gently into the lake. The cookies floated out to sea and the cream covered the spot so we could see nothing but soon it cleared up and we saw spoons, silver sugar tongs plus dishes in the sand below.

    Three of us donned our swimming suits and then the fun began - rescuing the silver, etc. The water was only 5 feet or so deep so we easily did surface dives and brought up spoons and tongs on our hands or even toes. Such fun we did have! It all received a first page column in the Tokyo paper the next day . . .

    'Berta"

MUSHROOMS ON A MOUNTAIN

"Grace is leaving in ten days . . .

Last Saturday we staff gave a picnic for her - all of us going out to Mino, a famous park an hour and a half from Kobe, climbing a small mountain and gathering mushrooms. That is the chief delight of the Japanese during this month and as neither of us had indulged we had great fun. A funny old man was our guide and he led us to the pine grove and showed us how with sticks we could brush away the dead leaves and find tender fresh mushrooms at the foot of the pines.

For our lunch two maids came up to where we were with food for a "torinabe," a mixture of chicken, bean curd (tofu), onions, mushrooms and vegetables all cooked together before us on charcoal braziers - a most delicious mixture when eaten on rice. At this picnic our rice even was filled with mushrooms and Oh, so yummy! We had climbed and hunted and ate late so the food disappeared quickly.

When we had finished we took pictures, then as we found a clearing we all had a dance - wood nymphs and that sort of thing! The Japanese in their beautiful kimonos are lovely when they sing and dance. Altogether it was a jolly time!"

CHRYSANTHEMUMS and MAPLE LEAVES

"Dear Mother and Father,
   Yesterday Helen, Lillian and I went to Nino to view the maple leaves. The water from Nino Falls has cut a deep gorge in its path to the sea and there are beautiful walks on both sides of the stream with lacy leafed maple trees overhanging. At this season some of the leaves are scarlet red, others a delicate yellow tint . . . We ate a Japanese lunch and for dessert had fried maple leaves. They were delicious! Try them sometime - fry in batter and deep fat."

". . . Most people in Japan right now are spending a great deal of time viewing the maples and going to the chrysanthemum shows. The Japanese Ladies Society entertained the Kobe Women's Club at a garden party at the home of Baroness Kawasaki the other day and I shall never forget the beauty of the Japanese garden with stone paths, tea houses, cedars in beautiful shapes and the display of huge chrysanthemums in all colors. Truly some of the flowers were as large as dinner plates and some as feathery as ostrich plumes, others firm and round. This particular garden is on the mountain side and the maples flaming red among the cedars were gorgeous."

". . . Yesterday we had an Association picnic above Nunobiki Falls and I simply cannot describe the colors we found as we wound among the mountains . . . At Sumadera we saw one plant with as many as 75 blossoms all in bloom and arranged with wire to make a street car . . . They also had old Japanese legends portrayed with the characters wearing costumes of chrysanthemums . . . very cleverly done."

THINKING ABOUT GOING HOME

"Dear Jae,

I have all my set now but dinner plates so can perhaps hold on to my money until I see just what I want and need. With only a year and a half left here I'm beginning to collect for myself now. I'm certain I'll not return so my Japanese things are becoming more precious."

"Jae dear,

. . . I'm really planning to go by ports when I leave . . . I want to stop in Java, go across India visiting the Taj Mahal, spend some time in Egypt and the Holy Land and a good bit in Italy. Doesn't that sound appealing? Coming out here to meet me and getting back to the states will only cost $1500. Do begin saving now for I can think of no one I'd rather travel with than you. Heaps of folks go second class - folks who can well afford to go first - so even if we did that we could have a grand time . . . When you get to Berkeley this summer and watch the liners head for Japan you'll just ache to run across to see me!"

"Dear Mother and Father,

..You ask if I'm not coming home soon? It looks as tho' I'll be staying my term out and returning via Siberia and Paris next summer (1931) reaching home in September or so . . .
    With dearest love to you both, Roberta"

GOING HOME

Roberta was aware from her parents' letters that her mother was coping with health problems, but her mother's death in July 1930 was totally unexpected. She immediately returned to Iowa.

ROBERTA RETURNS TO THE U.S.

After her ship docked in New York City, Roberta went directly to the home of her parents in Madrid, Iowa, where family and friends had gathered.

The Andersons were a close family, and in October Roberta wrote to her older brother, Paul, about their father:

". . . Paul, you don't know how glad I am that I came home immediately! I think just being here these few months . . . has given him a chance to get his bearings. Then too he's been so interested in my Japanese treasures and of course swells up with pride when I'm speaking anywhere that it takes his mind off himself. He needs to think of other things . . . and is just beginning to live a bit in the future."

NEXT STEPS
for
HARVEY and ROBERTA

THE YEARS AHEAD

When Roberta returned from Japan and she and Harvey looked at each other for the first time in four years, they realized their romance was real.

Harvey & Roberta Early 1930s

The Great Depression existed, however, but Harvey found an administrative position with the Wisconsin Electric Power Co. in Milwaukee; Roberta became a secretary with the Racine Y.W.C.A., ten miles south.

On February 6, 1932 they were married in the parlor of the home of Harvey's mother in Brandon and began their new life in Racine, where David and I were born. They later moved to Kenosha where Harvey's company transferred him.

To do good in the world continued as the fabric of their lives and they were involved in their community. Both Harvey and Roberta were active members of the First Methodist Church. They helped organize a program inviting foreign students at the University of Wisconsin Madison to spend a weekend staying in church members' homes. Foreign students thus experienced a U.S. community away from a college campus and Americans got acquainted with individuals from other countries and cultures.

In 1945 Harvey and Roberta bought five acres with a farmhouse near Kenosha. Harvey loved being close to the land. His vegetable garden provided food all year for our family, and he sold fresh vegetables to delighted staff at his office. The Smith Strawberry Farm - a family enterprise - was his successful idea to earn college money for David and me.

Family was important for Harvey and Roberta who encouraged our activities from 4-H through high school. We went to museum travel programs together and had Sunday evening bridge games. Trips to see Harvey's mother in Wisconsin and Roberta's family in Iowa were frequent.

Roberta created a weekly local radio program, "Your Home and You." She corresponded regularly with Japanese friends who visited Harvey and Roberta several times. After a student in the Bulgaria Trades School asked Harvey for help in applying for a job at Oregon State University College of Forestry, Harvey and Roberta visited him in Corvallis.

Harvey retired in 1958, created an apple orchard, and remained a "farmer at heart" on his land until his death in 1973 at age 87.

Roberta moved to Cedar Crest Retirement Home in Janesville, Wisconsin in the 1980s. She continued to write about her family as Swedish immigrants, and visited Sweden. She passed away in 1996 at age 95.

1970 in Apple Orchard

YMCA - YWCA
1920s and 2020s

The Y.M.C.A. and Y.W.C.A.
These organizations provided the opportunities for Harvey and Roberta to "do good in the world and have adventures."

 The equilateral triangle is a symbol of balance and harmony of the human spirit, mind and body.

The Young Men's Christian Association was founded in 1844 and the Young Women's Christian Association in 1855 in London. Both were concerned about the negative social conditions for young men and women working in the factories of the Industrial Revolution. They supported Christianity and the Christian principle of helping others. By the early 1900s they had expanded to other countries to address diverse needs.

Today both organizations welcome individuals of any or no faith, all races, genders and cultural/ethnic/national backgrounds. Neither organization now uses periods after its initials.

YMCA Today
"The YMCA believes in the unlimited potential of young people to use their ideas, talents and voice for the good."
"One Movement, One Collective Vision,
Many Approaches, United in Diversity"

YWCA Today
"YWCA is dedicated to eliminating racism, empowering women and promoting peace, justice, freedom and dignity for all."

Both organizations continue to be non-profit and non-governmental and supported by individuals and organizations.

www.worldymca.org   www.worldywca.org

The YMCA and YWCA each have local organizations in more than 120 countries which involve youth in (1) needs of their communities and (2) leadership on world issues.

The YMCA and YWCA both have World Offices in Geneva, Switzerland, which help publicize work in individual countries and organize youth participation in global programs.

Examples of Current YMCA Work in Countries
Projects are selected by local communities.
Job skills   Sports/fitness
Pre-schools   Leadership training
HIV/AIDS education   Street children

20th World Council Denmark July 2022
Purpose: Adoption of a World YMCA Vision 2030
Participants: 1000 in person in Denmark and 1500 on-line
Four pillars: Community and Wellbeing, Meaningful Work, A Sustainable Planet, A Just World

---

Examples of Current YWCA Work in Countries
Projects are selected by local communities.
Women's health   Leadership training
Immigrants, refugees   Women's entrepreneurship
Vocational training   Child marriage/labor

YW4A April 2022 - On going
Collaboration of 27 women's rights and faith-based organizations and 17,540 young women
in Egypt, Kenya, Palestine and South Sudan
to take individual and collective actions
for women's rights.

Current Status of the YMCA and YWCA in the Cities where Harvey and Roberta worked.

Vladivostok, Russia

In 1922 the Communists disbanded the Vladivostok Mayak-YMCA. There were no Y.M.C.A. associations in Russia for 74 years until 1996 when a Russian YMCA was established. Current programs, primarily in western Russia, include pre-school education, sports and fitness, a center for "street" children, theatre, and ecology. There is no YMCA in Vladivostok at this time.

Sofia, Bulgaria

After a half century break because of the communist government in Bulgaria, the YMCA began to revive in the 1990s. The YMCA is now in four cities including Sofia. The focus in Sofia is Art and Culture, and there are clubs of special interest, including puppet theatre and ceramics, summer youth camps, healthcare, leadership training, public service.

Kobe, Japan

The Kobe YWCA was formed in 1920 and has been an active organization ever since. Current programs include environmental actions, child raising, peace and human rights study, volunteers reading to blind persons, lunch meetings for the elderly, support for homeless individuals and Christian study.

The Kobe YWCA College evolved from the Japanese language classes taught by the YWCA in the 1920s, and now offers a variety of courses in the Japanese language.

ACKNOWLEDGEMENTS

My sincere thanks to all of my talented family and friends for their insights and perspective.

My brother David and his wife Barbara supported this project from the very beginning with ideas and enthusiasm. My husband, John, an author, shared his knowledge and read every draft—and there were many. Cousins Mary Glenn and daughter Barbara contributed family history and Karen West her editing skills. Ariyoshi Okumura, the son of Japanese friends Roberta knew in the 1920s and his son, Yutaka Okumura, shared their knowledge.

My thanks to special friends on San Juan Island who were integral to this book's progression and completion—you each know how much you contributed and how appreciative I am: Karin Agosta, Julia Ashirov, Carolyn Haugen, Robin Jacobson, Wendy Shepard, Lori Stokes, Lee Sturdivant, Janet Thomas, Jean Thomas, Gerard Woldtvedt.

W. Bruce Conway, WBC Design in Friday Harbor, designed the book layout and cover.

Jim Maya, Maya's Images in Friday Harbor, took my photo for this book holding onion skin letters.

Archives
Smith College
YWCA Special Collections, Northampton, MA

University of Minnesota
Kautz Family YMCA Archives, Minneapolis, MN

University of Southern California
YMCA Archives, Mark L. Moody Collection, Los Angeles, CA

APPENDIX

Definitions of Japanese Words in Roberta's Letters

The Diet	Japan's national legislature composed of House of Representatives and the House of Councillors.
furoshiki	Traditional square Japanese cloth used to wrap gifts or carry goods or packages
geta	Traditional wooden shoe, elevated from the ground, with two straps from the front so the big toe in tabi hooks into one side
guynabe	Onions, mushrooms, beef steak with shoyu on top of rice and more. p. 246
haori	Traditional Japanese hip or thigh length jacket worn over a kimono
Kanjo	Roberta's reference to household accounting
Mainichi	Japan's oldest newspaper
obi	A long broad sash tied in a large flat bow at the back and worn around the waist of a kimono
omiyage	A Japanese tradition of bringing a gift or souvenir to give to friends, co-workers and family after returning from a trip
osushi	Rice with mushrooms, green string beans and garnished with red fish grated and more. p.177
ri	2.5 miles
shoyu	soy sauce
tabi	A white stocking that comes to the ankle made with a place for the big toe for wearing geta.
Takuhon	Japanese langage textbook
yen	Japanese currency
Yokan	Sweet snack bars usually eaten in slices or in small blocks as dessert
zori	Traditional Japanese sandals

BIBLIOGRAPHY

Anderson, Paul B. *No East or West. YMCA-Press*, 1985.

Baird, Catherine. *Revolution From Within.* Atlanta. *Book Logix, 2013.*

Boyd, Nancy. *Emissaries: Overseas Work of the American YWCA 1895-1970.* New York. *The Woman's Press, 1986.*

Crampton, R.J. A *Short History of Modern Bulgaria.* Great Britain. *Cambridge University Press,* 1987.

Mason, R.H.P., Caiger, J.G. *A History of Japan, Revised Edition.* China. *Tuttle Publishing, 1997.*

Miller, Matthew L. *The American YMCA and Russian Culture.* Lanham, MD. *Lexington Books*, 2013.

Milner, et al. *Japan 15th Edition.* Singapore, *Lonely Planet Global Limited,* 2017.

Rice, Anna V. *A History of the World's Young Women's Christian Association.* New York. *The Woman's Press.* 1947.

Salisbury, Harrison E. *Black Night, White Snow: Russia's Revolutions 1905-1917.* New York. *Doubleday & Co. 1978.*

Smith, Canfield F. V*ladivostok Under Red and White Rule Revolution and Counterrevolution in the Russian Far East 1920-1922.* Seattle. *University of Washington Press, 1975.*

Bryn Thomas & Daniel McCrohan *Trans-Siberian Handbook 10th Edition.* Surrey, UK. *Trailblazer Publications,* 2019.

ABOUT THE AUTHOR

I was fortunate to grow up in a Wisconsin home with the world part of my life: a Russian samovar, a carved bench from Bulgaria, and a Japanese kakemono, a hanging artistic scroll, on the living room wall.

My four years at the University of Wisconsin in Madison were exciting with challenging liberal arts classes, a sociology major and participation in campus activities.

An M.A. at Northwestern University in sociology was next with a grant for research in Jamaica.

With letters written a century ago.

Then a move West which had always been my dream: first as Activities Adviser at Chico State and San Francisco State colleges, and in the 1960s as an Associate Dean in the Dean of Students Office, University of California, Berkeley.

A desire for rural life led to the Northwest and San Juan Island and I became counselor at our island high school for 18 years. Each of my positions I consider special because students and I were sharing ideas and options—always a challenge and a delight.

Another dream came true: I had my own horse. We competed in the barrel races at the San Juan County Fair as members of the "Over the Hill Gang" for riders age 40 and over.

After 1990, my life took a different direction. Instead of working with students, I started working with words. From 1991 to 2007, I wrote and published ten editions of *Emily's Guide & Maps to the San Juan Islands,* and for several years wrote a monthly column in *The Islands Weekly,* a local newspaper, profiling island artists. Then—boxes of letters and this book.

I hope you find my parents' experiences a century ago in Bulgaria, Japan and Russia engaging and enlightening.